I0012847

Regularized Optimization Methods
for Reconstruction and Modeling
in Computer Graphics

Von der Carl-Friedrich-Gauß-Fakultät

der Technischen Universität Carolo-Wilhelmina zu Braunschweig

zur Erlangung des Grades eines

Doktoringenieurs (Dr.-Ing.)

genehmigte Dissertation

von

Stephan Paul Wenger

geboren am 19. März 1986

in Salzgitter

Eingereicht am:	4. April 2014
Disputation am:	17. Juni 2014
1. Referent:	Prof. Dr.-Ing. Marcus Magnor
2. Referent:	Prof. Dr. Rüdiger Westermann

(2014)

Stephan Wenger:

Regularized Optimization Methods

for Reconstruction and Modeling

in Computer Graphics

© 2014 Stephan Wenger

Satz und Umschlag: Stephan Wenger

Illustrationen: siehe Seite 179

Herstellung und Verlag: BoD – Books on Demand, Norderstedt

ISBN 978-3-7357-4299-5

Abstract

The field of computer graphics deals with virtual representations of the real world. These can be obtained either through *reconstruction* of a model from measurements, or by directly *modeling* a virtual object, often on a real-world example. The former is often formalized as a regularized optimization problem, in which a data term ensures consistency between model and data and a regularization term promotes solutions that have high a priori probability.

In this dissertation, different reconstruction problems in computer graphics are shown to be instances of a common class of optimization problems which can be solved using a uniform algorithmic framework. Moreover, it is shown that similar optimization methods can also be used to solve data-based modeling problems, where the amount of information that can be obtained from measurements is insufficient for accurate reconstruction.

As real-world examples of reconstruction problems, sparsity and group sparsity methods are presented for radio interferometric image reconstruction in static and time-dependent settings. As a modeling example, analogous approaches are investigated to automatically create volumetric models of astronomical nebulae from single images based on symmetry assumptions.

Zusammenfassung

Das Feld der Computergraphik beschäftigt sich mit virtuellen Abbildern der realen Welt. Diese können erlangt werden durch *Rekonstruktion* eines Modells aus Messdaten, oder durch direkte *Modellierung* eines virtuellen Objekts, oft nach einem realen Vorbild. Ersteres wird oft als regularisiertes Optimierungsproblem dargestellt, in dem ein Datenterm die Konsistenz zwischen Modell und Daten sicherstellt, während ein Regularisierungsterm Lösungen fördert, die eine hohe A-priori-Wahrscheinlichkeit aufweisen.

In dieser Arbeit wird gezeigt, dass verschiedene Rekonstruktionsprobleme der Computergraphik Instanzen einer gemeinsamen Klasse von Optimierungsproblemen sind, die mit einem einheitlichen algorithmischen Framework gelöst werden können. Darüber hinaus wird gezeigt, dass vergleichbare Optimierungsverfahren auch genutzt werden können, um Probleme der datenbasierten Modellierung zu lösen, bei denen die aus Messungen verfügbaren Daten nicht für eine genaue Rekonstruktion ausreichen.

Als praxisrelevante Beispiele für Rekonstruktionsprobleme werden Sparsity- und Group-Sparsity-Methoden für die radiointerferometrische Bildrekonstruktion im statischen und zeitabhängigen Fall vorgestellt. Als Beispiel für Modellierung werden analoge Verfahren untersucht, um basierend auf Symmetrieannahmen automatisch volumetrische Modelle astronomischer Nebel aus Einzelbildern zu erzeugen.

Acknowledgments

This work would not have been possible without the help of many people: first of all, my advisor Prof. Dr.-Ing. Marcus Magnor, whose ideas provided the basis for most of my research and whose constant support kept me going, and Prof. Dr. Dirk Lorenz, who repeatedly shared his immense knowledge about optimization methods with me and spawned many fruitful ideas in the process. I am also grateful for the enjoyable collaborations and fertile discussions with Prof. Ylva Pihlström from UNM as well as Sanjay Bhatnagar and Urvashi Rau from NRAO (about radio interferometry), with Soheil Darabi and Prof. Pradeep Sen from UNM as well as Andreas Tillmann from TU Darmstadt (about compressed sensing), and with Marco Ament and Prof. Daniel Weiskopf from Stuttgart University (about astronomical nebula reconstruction).

I further have to thank Martin Eisemann for his postdoc advice and his constant cheerfulness in the lab, Lorenz Rogge for being the most likeable and witty office mate I could have wished for, and the whole crowd at the *Institut für Computergraphik* who provided me with a lot of fun, advice when needed, and a great working atmosphere for over six years. Special thanks go to Thomas Neumann for sharing my enthusiasm with both optimization techniques and the Python programming language, and for our continuous and inspiring exchange of ideas.

Moreover, I would like to thank Michael Stengel for helping create illustrations for this dissertation, and Marcus Magnor, Martin Eisemann, Thomas Neumann, Dirk Lorenz, and Pablo Bauszat for proofreading. All remaining errors are, of course, solely my own responsibility.

Contents

Preface

This dissertation is based on several publications I have authored in cooperation with different co-authors. In my dissertation, these publications are presented in the common context of regularized optimization methods. The text incorporates material, such as figures, data, plots, and text passages, from my published work. My advisor Prof. Dr.-Ing. Marcus Magnor is a co-author on all of my publications, for which he provided ideas and advice. The individual contributions of all other authors to the works incorporated in the dissertation are clarified in the following.

The basic interferometric reconstruction algorithm presented in Section 3.3 was developed in the context of my diploma thesis in physics [Wen10]. It is recapitulated in Chapter 3 as a foundation for the subsequent chapters, reusing material from the thesis. My work led to a technical report [WM10] as well as to a publication in a peer-reviewed journal [WMP+10] together with Ylva Pihlström, Sanjay Bhatnagar, and Urvashi Rau. Ylva Pihlström inducted me in the basics of radio astronomy and produced reference images using CLEAN.

Sanjay Bhatnagar and Urvashi Rau provided experimental data as well as an introduction to radio interferometry and the Casa software package. The experimental setup, implementation, and evaluation as well as the texts of the publications are my own work.

The analysis of the role of randomness in the context of radio interferometric sampling, Section 3.5, was joint work with Soheil Darabi, Pradeep Sen, and Karl-Heinz Glaßmeier [WDS+10]. Soheil Darabi and Pradeep Sen pointed me to the relevant literature on compressed sensing and provided valuable feedback and discussion, while Karl-Heinz Glaßmeier provided general advice. The experimental setup, implementation, and evaluation as well as the paper itself are my own work.

The symmetry-based modeling algorithm for volumetric data, Chapter 4, was joint work with Marco Ament, Stefan Guthe, Dirk Lorenz, Andreas Tillmann, and Daniel Weiskopf [WAG+12]. I conceived the idea, created the prototype implementation, and wrote most of the paper. Stefan Guthe contributed a parallel raycasting algorithm and the corresponding section in the paper. Marco Ament contributed the parallel implementation based on my code as well as the corresponding section and illustrations in the paper. He also ran the reconstruction algorithm on the University of Stuttgart's multi-GPU cluster to produce results with varying parameters and the corresponding performance statistics. Dirk Lorenz and Andreas Tillmann helped with the selection of an appropriate optimization algorithm. Jittering of the symmetry axis originated from discussions with Marco Ament; hard constraints and the spatially varying regularization parameter emerged during discussions with Dirk Lorenz. Daniel Weiskopf provided supervision and general advice. In addition, Michael Stengel helped produce the three-dimensional illustrations in the paper.

The group sparsity reconstruction algorithm for interferometric data, Chapter 5, was joint work with Urvashi Rau [WRM13a; WRM13b]. She provided radio telescope data, reference reconstructions using MS-CLEAN and MS-TV-CLEAN, and their descriptions in the paper, as well as information on time-varying signals and related work. The idea was conceived during a discussion with Dirk Lorenz. The design and implementation as well as the evaluation and presentation are my own work.

The group sparsity modeling approach for volumetric data, Chapter 6, was joint work with Dirk Lorenz [WLM13], who provided valuable information on group sparsity algorithms. The idea, algorithm design and implementation as well as evaluation and presentation are my own work.

In addition to these publications, I have authored or co-authored several publications that are loosely related to this dissertation and may provide additional insight into certain aspects of the present work or a wider overview of its field of application: a method for algebraic reconstruction of symmetric volumetric objects [AFWMM08; WAFMM09]; an approach to the semi-automatic modeling of astronomical nebulae from single images [Wen09; WMSM09]; an interactive modeling tool for astronomical objects [SKW+11; WSK+10]; high-level overviews of problems and techniques in reconstruction and modeling of volumetric phenomena [MSK+10; WAS+12]; a method for editing volumetric data sets [RWF+13]; and novel algorithms for optimization problems that occur in symmetry-based modeling [LSW14; LWSM14].

I have further authored or co-authored several publications in other fields not directly related to the topic of this dissertation. These publications are listed here for completeness: a shape-from-shading algorithm for reconstruction of the lunar surface [WSSM09]; a C++ library for intuitive GPU programming [WWM11]; several works on audio resynthesis [TWM13a; TWM13b; WM11; WM12]; an EEG-based evaluation of artifacts in video [LWM11]; a simple portable multi-view camera design [WJM12]; an algorithm for apparent resolution enhancement in videos [SEW+13]; and a method for finding meaningful basis functions for the representation of mesh animations [NVW+13].

Notation

In the following, matrices and vectors are written in bold typeface: $\mathbf{M}$, $\mathbf{x}$. Lower right indices denote components of a vector: x_i. Often, multi-dimensional arrays are interpreted as vectors; in this case, multiple indices can be present: $x_{i,j}$. Sometimes, several components of a vector have to be extracted, yielding a new vector; this is represented by an *index set* as a lower right index, in square brackets: $\mathbf{x}_{[g]}$. When quantities change during the steps of an iterative algorithm, the step is indicated as an upper right index in parentheses: $\mathbf{x}^{(k)}$.

$\min \mathbf{x}$, $\max \mathbf{x}$, and $\sum \mathbf{x}$ denote the minimum, maximum, and sum of the components of a vector or set $\mathbf{x}$. The minimum and maximum of two scalars v and w are written $\min(v, w)$ and $\max(v, w)$; equivalently, $\min(\mathbf{v}, \mathbf{w})$ and $\max(\mathbf{v}, \mathbf{w})$ denote the element-wise minimum and maximum of two vectors $\mathbf{v}$ and $\mathbf{w}$ (or, analogously, a vector and a scalar). The element-wise absolute values of the components of a vector $\mathbf{x}$ are written $|\mathbf{x}|$; for sets, $|\cdot|$ denotes the cardinality, the number of elements in the set. The signum function $\operatorname{sgn} x = x / |x|$ returns the sign of x (or 0 for $x = 0$), and acts element-wise on vectors. x^{T} denotes the transpose, x^* the complex conjugate.

$\|\mathbf{x}\|_p$ denotes the ℓ_p-norm of $\mathbf{x}$, $\|\mathbf{x}\|_p = \left(\sum_i |x_i|^p\right)^{1/p}$. Common choices for p include 1, 2, and ∞ ($\|\mathbf{x}\|_\infty = \max |\mathbf{x}|$). The number of nonzero components is written $\|\mathbf{x}\|_0$.

A glossary of recurring quantities can be found on page 177.

1 Introduction

A major goal of computer graphics is to create realistic virtual representations of the real world. Examples of such representations include images, light fields, textured polygon meshes, or volumetric models. They are captured using a variety of instruments and techniques: cameras, camera arrays, 3D scanners, computed tomography scanners, depth cameras, and many more.

In many cases, capturing the complete information needed to accurately represent a scene is difficult or infeasible: a camera has limited resolution and thus inevitably loses high image frequencies. A computed tomography scanner can only capture a small number of projections in order not to endanger the patient. A radio interferometer records only a sparse subset of spatial frequencies. In such cases, a *reconstruction* method has to make up for the missing information in order to create a complete model of the real world.

In the aforementioned cases, it is (in principle) possible to collect more data to improve the quality of the reconstruction. However, there are situations when it is fundamentally impossible to gather any noteworthy fraction of the data. For example, some astronomical objects are so far away that only one projection can ever be observed from within our solar system. The data needed for a complete volumetric reconstruction can therefore not be acquired from Earth, regardless of the instrument used and the effort made. Still, one can try to create models that are physically and perceptually *plausible*, i.e., that are compatible with known physical principles, consistent with the observed data, and free from visual artifacts. Creating a plausible model from such vastly incomplete data is an extremely ill-posed problem, and any "reconstruction" algorithm needs to make up the better part of the result without any guaranteed bounds for the discrepancy between model and reality. Because the results in this case depend more on the algorithm than on the observational data, it would not be completely accurate to call this task a *reconstruction* problem; instead, I refer to it as *data-based modeling* to emphasize the difference to traditional, more tractable inverse problems that are *reconstruction* problems in the strict sense. Because of the similarity of the underlying methods and algorithms, however, I will often use the terms "reconstruction" and "data-based modeling" interchangeably when referring to data-based modeling problems.

In both reconstruction and data-based modeling, a reconstruction algorithm requires prior assumptions about the expected structure of the data to fill in the missing information: in a computed tomography setting, this might include the assumptions that neighboring voxel cells have similar densities, that most voxels are empty, and that non-empty cells are most likely to be found in the center of the volume. In an image reconstruction problem, one can make use of the fact that natural images are often sparse in some wavelet representation. In an astronomical modeling problem, the missing third dimension can often be inferred from an image by exploiting the fact that certain astronomical nebulae are approximately symmetric.

Both reconstruction and data-based modeling are *inverse problems*, which are ubiquitous in computer graphics [Kas92]: for example, to-mographic approaches are used for image-based volumetric reconstruction of trees [RMMD04; VGS+12], flames [IM04], gas flows [AIH+08; BAI+09; BRA+11; IBA+09], and fluids [GKHH12]. Tomographic data-based modeling with highly incomplete or inconsistent data is employed for the creation of static light-field displays [WLHR11] and as a basic paradigm for manual volume modeling [KISE13]. Regularized optimization techniques are also applied to computational photography [HRH+13; SD09] and stochastic ray-tracing [KS13; SD10; SD11; SDX11]. Another interesting example of data-based modeling using regularized optimization methods is the automatic generation of meaningful deformation basis functions from recorded mesh animations [NVW+13].

Such inverse problems can be solved using *regularized optimization methods*. The task at hand is to find the *most plausible* signal vector $\mathbf{x}$ that is consistent with the observed data $\mathbf{y}$. Since captured data often contains noise, small deviations from the data are typically allowed in favor of a more plausible solution. The resulting *denoising* problem consists of a *data term* that enforces consistency with the observed data and a *regularizer* that promotes plausibility according to a priori assumptions about the result. The regularizer not only has to describe the expected solution well; it also needs to be able to discriminate between different possible solutions, i.e., it must be sufficiently *orthogonal* or *incoherent* to the information provided by the measurement. If these assumptions are fulfilled, solving the optimization problem is likely to yield a good representation of the real world phenomenon.

In this thesis, regularized optimization methods are applied to two very different use cases within the field of computer graphics: reconstruction problems from radio interferometry and modeling problems regarding astronomical nebulae. Both classes of problems are approached with two different types of regularizers, first with simple sparsity-inducing regularizers, then with more advanced group sparsity methods:

	radio interferometry *reconstruction*	astronomical nebula *modeling*
sparsity	Chapter 3	Chapter 4
group sparsity	Chapter 5	Chapter 6

While the basic structure of the underlying optimization problems is very similar, the major challenge consists in finding suitable regularizers tailored to the respective problems and in implementing appropriate algorithms that are able to handle the—often considerable—amounts of data associated with these problems.

The following chapter provides an overview of the theoretical background of my work as well as an introduction to the optimization algorithms on which later chapters build. Chapters 3 to 6 present the different applications, including relevant background, related work, algorithms, results, and discussion. An overall conclusion and outlook are given in Chapter 7.

2 Theoretical Background

Many physical measurement methods are—at least approximately—linear. That means that the measured data vector $\mathbf{y}$ depends on the internal state of the system, the signal vector $\mathbf{x}$, in a linear way, so that the measurement process can be written as a system of linear equations,

$$\mathbf{y} = \mathbf{Mx} \,. \tag{2.1}$$

This model includes, for example, digital cameras, where each image pixel is an integral over a solid angle of light from the scene, as well as radio interferometers, Chapters 3 and 5, which sample an image in the Fourier domain. Purely emissive (additive) volume rendering, Chapters 4 and 6, also falls in this category. Even computed tomography can be covered: although X-ray intensity decreases exponentially with the thickness of an absorbing layer, the image formation process is linear in log-space.

An actual physical measurement will often contain noise in addition to the data. This noise is typically modeled as an additive noise vector σ with independent, normally distributed components, so that

$$\mathbf{y} = \mathbf{Mx} + \sigma \; . \tag{2.2}$$

In the absence of noise, in order to recover the signal $\mathbf{x}$ from the measurement $\mathbf{y}$, the linear measurement operator $\mathbf{M}$ would have to be inverted. In some cases, $\mathbf{M}$ has full rank, so the inversion is directly possible. In other cases, the information in $\mathbf{y}$ does not suffice to uniquely determine $\mathbf{x}$; additional information must then be provided, typically in form of a *regularizer*, to select the most plausible $\mathbf{x}$ from all those consistent with the measured data. This is generally the case in Chapters 3, 5, and 6, and, to some extent, in Chapter 4. Even if the information in $\mathbf{y}$ is complete but noisy, regularized reconstruction can often recover the support of the signal $\mathbf{x}$ *exactly* (together with an approximation of the signal components) if appropriate assumptions about its structure are available.

2.1 Compressed sensing

The conditions under which exact recovery from incomplete measurements is possible have only recently been extensively studied, providing the foundations for a general mathematical theory of sampling now known as *compressed sensing* [Don06], *compressive sensing* [Bar07], *compressive sampling* [Can06], or simply "CS". The name refers to the fact that with a suitable choice of measurement basis, perfect reconstruction is often possible at sampling rates way below the "classical" Shannon–Nyquist limit; the captured signal $\mathbf{y}$ is therefore a *compressed* representation of the signal $\mathbf{x}$. Compression that is traditionally applied *after* a measurement—for example, JPEG compression of an image—here becomes *part* of the measurement. Compressed sensing theory provides the foundations for the reconstruction approach presented in Chapter 3 and the inspiration for the methods described in the subsequent chapters.

2.1.1 Relation to classical sampling theory

In Shannon–Nyquist theory, it is assumed that the signal $\mathbf{x}$ is *band-limited*, i.e., its Fourier representation only contains frequencies below a given threshold. The signal is then sampled in the time domain with a fixed sampling frequency. Compressed sensing, however, allows for *any* linear measurement basis $\mathbf{M}$ and assumes that the signal $\mathbf{x}$ is *sparse*, i.e., most coefficients of $\mathbf{x}$ are zero. It is generally not required to know which or even how many entries of $\mathbf{x}$ are nonzero.

2.1.2 Sparsity bases

In many cases, $\mathbf{x}$ is not immediately sparse in its most obvious (observable) representation. However, an appropriate basis $\mathbf{S}$ may exist such that $\mathbf{x}$ becomes sparse when represented in that basis. In this case,

$$\mathbf{x} = \mathbf{S}\mathbf{s} \,, \tag{2.3}$$

for some sparse vector $\mathbf{s}$.

The appropriate choice of $\mathbf{S}$ depends strongly on the type of signal. Common sparsity bases for natural images are, for example, the various wavelet transforms [DJL92]; or a time series of amplitudes from a radio receiver might be sparse in the frequency domain, indicating the distinct frequency bands used for communication.

If a sparsity basis is given, the measurement equation (2.2) becomes

$$\mathbf{y} = \mathbf{M}\mathbf{S}\mathbf{s} \,. \tag{2.4}$$

Since this can be interpreted as a measurement of a different (sparse) signal $\mathbf{s}$ with a different measurement matrix $\mathbf{M}' = \mathbf{M}\mathbf{S}$, the following discussion will only consider the case where $\mathbf{x}$ is sparse, without any loss of generality.

2.1.3 Reconstruction

Compressed sensing states that under certain assumptions about the measurement matrix $\mathbf{M}$, reconstructing a sparse $\mathbf{x}$ from a measurement $\mathbf{y}$ is possible by computing the *sparsest* $\mathbf{x}$ that satisfies $\mathbf{y} = \mathbf{M}\mathbf{x}$, i.e.,

$$\mathbf{x}_{\text{reconstructed}} = \arg\min_{\mathbf{x}} \|\mathbf{x}\|_0 \quad \text{subject to} \quad \mathbf{y} = \mathbf{M}\mathbf{x} \,. \tag{2.5}$$

Here, $\|\mathbf{x}\|_0$ is the so-called ℓ_0-norm of $\mathbf{x}$, the number of nonzero components in the vector $\mathbf{x}$; a signal containing at most s nonzero components is said to be s-*sparse*.

Unfortunately, solving (2.5) is a combinatorial problem, and is in fact NP-hard [GJY11]. In high dimensions, however, it is increasingly probable that the same result can be obtained by minimizing the ℓ_1-norm $\|\mathbf{x}\|_1 = \sum_i |x_i|$ instead of the ℓ_0-norm [CRT06a], leading to the computationally much more accessible problem

$$\mathbf{x}_{\text{reconstructed}} = \arg\min_{\mathbf{x}} \|\mathbf{x}\|_1 \quad \text{subject to} \quad \mathbf{y} = \mathbf{M}\mathbf{x}\,, \qquad (2.6)$$

commonly referred to as *basis pursuit* [CDS98].

2.1.4 Conditions for perfect reconstruction

A general condition for the possibility of perfect reconstruction of $\mathbf{x}$ from $\mathbf{y}$ using (2.6) is that the measurement basis and the sparsity basis are sufficiently *incoherent* [Don06]. Graphically speaking, this means that the information from nonzero entries of $\mathbf{x}$ is spread out across many components of $\mathbf{y}$. For example, even if an image contains only very few nonzero pixels, each sampled spatial frequency provides information about all of these pixels (the Fourier transform of a Dirac pulse has infinite support). Thus, it is rather unlikely that different (sufficiently sparse) signals produce the same set of (sufficiently complete) measurements, and recovering the sparsest signal

11

compatible with the measurements will very probably reproduce the correct signal. On the contrary, if the signal was sampled in the spatial domain instead of the frequency domain, most samples would contain very little information ("this pixel is not one of the nonzero pixels"), and perfect reconstruction would be impossible from most random samplings. In fact, any pixel not "accidentally" sampled would be completely undefined. Apparently, the Fourier representation is "very orthogonal" to the pixel representation, while the pixel representation is "not orthogonal" to itself.

This notion can be quantified by introducing two *restricted isometry constants* that measure how closely the columns of $\mathbf{M}$ resemble an orthonormal system when acting on s-sparse vectors [CT05]. The first is the smallest δ_s such that

$$(1 - \delta_s) \left\| \mathbf{x} \right\|_2^2 \leq \left\| \mathbf{M}\mathbf{x} \right\|_2^2 \leq (1 + \delta_s) \left\| \mathbf{x} \right\|_2^2 \qquad (2.7)$$

for all $\mathbf{x}$ with at most s nonzero components. If δ_s is sufficiently small, only very little information is lost by measuring an s-sparse $\mathbf{x}$ using $\mathbf{M}$. In fact, if $\delta_{2s} < 1$, any $\mathbf{x}$ with at most s nonzero components can in principle be reconstructed from $\mathbf{y} = \mathbf{M}\mathbf{x}$ [CT05, Lemma 1.3]. However, this reconstruction might require enumerating all possible sparsity patterns, which is computationally intractable. The possibility of recovering $\mathbf{x}$ using ℓ_1 minimization can be verified by defining a second constant $\theta_{s,s'}$ such that

$$\left|(\mathbf{M}\mathbf{x})^{\mathsf{T}}\mathbf{M}\mathbf{x}'\right| \leq \theta_{s,s'}\left\|\mathbf{x}\right\|_2\left\|\mathbf{x}'\right\|_2 \tag{2.8}$$

for all $\mathbf{x}$ and $\mathbf{x}'$ with *disjoint* sets of at most s and s' nonzero components, respectively. It quantifies how much cross-talk between components of $\mathbf{x}$ is introduced by $\mathbf{M}$. If orthogonal $\mathbf{x}$ and $\mathbf{x}'$ remain orthogonal even after applying $\mathbf{M}$, they can still be discriminated by looking at the respective measurements $\mathbf{y} = \mathbf{M}\mathbf{x}$ and $\mathbf{y}' = \mathbf{M}\mathbf{x}'$. More precisely, if $\delta_s + \theta_{s,s} + \theta_{s,2s} < 1$, s-sparse $\mathbf{x}$ can be reconstructed from $\mathbf{y}$ by solving (2.6) [CT05, theorem 1.4].

How probable is it that any given matrix $\mathbf{M}$ fulfills such a *restricted isometry property*? It can be shown [Can06] that if $\mathbf{M}$ is a randomly sampled Fourier transform and the n-dimensional signal $\mathbf{x}$ is s-sparse, the probability of perfect reconstruction from k frequency samples chosen uniformly at random exceeds

$$\mathcal{P}(k) = 1 - \mathcal{O}(e^{\log n - k/22s})\,. \tag{2.9}$$

Similar results can be obtained for other random $\mathbf{M}$, for example, with independent and identically normally distributed components [CT06].

2.1.5 Stability and robustness

Under the aforementioned conditions, (2.6) provides perfect reconstruction for a completely noise-free measurement. Since real physical measurements, such as the interferometric measurements discussed in

Chapters 3 and 5, often contain noise, it is sometimes more realistic to relax the constraint to allow for a specified amount $\|\sigma\|_2$ of noise, so that the problem becomes [CRT06b]

$$\mathbf{x}_{\text{reconstructed}} = \arg\min_{\mathbf{x}} \|\mathbf{x}\|_1 \quad \text{s.t.} \quad \|\mathbf{Mx} - \mathbf{y}\|_2 \leq \|\sigma\|_2 \ . \quad (2.10)$$

The solution of this problem is stable with respect to noise, i.e., the error in the reconstruction is at most proportional to the error in the measurement $\mathbf{y}$. It is also stable with respect to imperfect sparsity of $\mathbf{x}$: if $\mathbf{x}$ is not sparse, as is the case in many practical applications, the result will be close to a vector containing only the largest components of $\mathbf{x}$ [CRT06b].

Instead of solving (2.10) directly, it is often more convenient to replace the hard constraint with a "soft" data term, such that

$$\mathbf{x}_{\text{reconstructed}} = \arg\min_{\mathbf{x}} \tfrac{1}{2} \|\mathbf{Mx} - \mathbf{y}\|_2^2 + \lambda \|\mathbf{x}\|_1 \ , \quad (2.11)$$

known as *basis pursuit denoising* [CDS98]. Any nontrivial solution of (2.10) is also a minimizer of (2.11) for some λ [FNW07]. In particular, as $\lambda \to 0$, the solution of (2.11) converges towards a solution of (2.6) [GSH11]. For normally distributed noise, λ can be derived from $\|\sigma\|_2$ in the context of a maximum a posteriori estimation method [CCPW07, remark 3.6]. In practice, it is often sufficient to approximate λ to within a few orders of magnitude, and to re-run the algorithm with a different λ if the noise constraint in (2.10) is violated. Even if the amount of noise is unknown (or if there is no defined noise level, as is the case in a modeling problem as opposed to a reconstruction problem), λ provides some intuitive control over the magnitude of regularization.

2.1.6 General regularizers

The theoretical foundations for ℓ_1-norm regularized reconstruction methods are well studied, and such methods have been successfully applied to a wide range of problems. However, many related problems are not easily expressed in the ℓ_1-norm formalism. In such cases, a more general formalism is often used in which the ℓ_1-norm is replaced by a general regularization term $f(\mathbf{x})$, so that (2.11) becomes

$$\arg \min_{\mathbf{x}} \tfrac{1}{2} \left\| \mathbf{Mx} - \mathbf{y} \right\|_2^2 + \lambda f(\mathbf{x}) \ . \tag{2.12}$$

While the theoretical results regarding the probability of perfect reconstruction cannot, in general, be transferred to this more general formulation, it has proven useful in a wide range of applications. One such application are *group sparsity* problems [FR08; WNF09], where joint activation of certain groups of signal components is promoted. Chapters 5 and 6 build on this idea. In group sparsity problems, the vector $\mathbf{x}$ is decomposed into several disjoint vectors $\mathbf{x}_{[g]}$, where each g is a set of indices, and G is the set of all g used in the decomposition of $\mathbf{x}$. The regularizer is written as a sum of contributions from these $\mathbf{x}_{[g]}$,

$$f(\mathbf{x}) = \sum_{g \in G} f_g(\mathbf{x}_{[g]}) \; . \tag{2.13}$$

Such a regularizer is called *separable*, as the different *groups g* can be handled independently during many stages of the algorithm. Group sparsity regularizers can be used if different components of $\mathbf{x}$ are likely to be *jointly* activated: for example, in color image restoration, it could make sense to assume that an image gradient in a given pixel is either zero or nonzero in all color channels simultaneously. In Chapters 5 and 6, f_g is chosen as the ℓ_∞-norm; the ℓ_2-norm is another popular choice [BVN07a; BVN07b; MÇW05]. A special case of group sparsity regularizers is the *total variation* (TV) [CD09; Cha04]

$$TV(\mathbf{x}) = \sum_{i,j} \|(\nabla \mathbf{x})_{i,j}\|_2 \; , \tag{2.14}$$

which promotes piece-wise constant solutions and is thus well suited for images with sharp edges and little texture, a typical situation in medical imaging.

2.2 Proximal algorithms

Optimization problems like (2.12) often cannot be solved using common gradient-based optimization methods because typical choices for f, like the ℓ_1-norm used in Chapters 3 and 4, are not everywhere differentiable. However, there is a class of algorithms that efficiently minimizes even nondifferentiable functions, as long as they are closed, proper, and convex (i.e., $\{(\mathbf{x}, c) \mid f(\mathbf{x}) \leq c\}$ is a nonempty closed convex set). These *proximal algorithms* [PB13] are based on evaluating the *proximal mapping* (or *proximity operator*)

$$p_f(\mathbf{x}) = \arg\min_{\mathbf{w}} \tfrac{1}{2} \|\mathbf{w} - \mathbf{x}\|_2^2 + f(\mathbf{w}) , \qquad (2.15)$$

which finds a point $\mathbf{w}$ that is not far from $\mathbf{x}$, but closer to the minimum of f. Often, f is weighted with a "step size" β,

$$p_{\beta f}(\mathbf{x}) = \arg\min_{\mathbf{w}} \tfrac{1}{2} \|\mathbf{w} - \mathbf{x}\|_2^2 + \beta f(\mathbf{w}) , \qquad (2.16)$$

where larger values of β move $\mathbf{w}$ farther in the direction of the minimum.

Proximal mappings can be better understood by considering the following two special cases. If f is an *indicator function*, i.e., there is a set C such that $f(\mathbf{x}) = 0$ for $\mathbf{x} \in C$ and ∞ otherwise, the proximal mapping is the orthogonal projection onto that C. If, on the other hand, f is differentiable, then $p_{\beta f}(\mathbf{x}) \approx \mathbf{x} - \beta \nabla f(\mathbf{x})$ for small β. Applying the proximal mapping can therefore be interpreted as a generalization of both gradient descent methods and projections on the feasible set.

2.2.1 Proximal gradient methods

It is easy to see that fixed points of p_f (or $p_{\beta f}$, for $\beta > 0$) are minimizers of f. If the proximal mapping can be computed efficiently for a given f, repeatedly applying p_f minimizes even nonsmooth functions like the ℓ_1-norm. However, minimizing (2.12) requires minimizing not only f, but a problem of the form

$$\arg\min_{\mathbf{x}} d(\mathbf{x}) + f(\mathbf{x}) \,. \tag{2.17}$$

In the applications investigated in the following chapters, the data term d and the regularizer f are closed proper convex functions and d is differentiable. A simple algorithm solving (2.17) is the *proximal gradient method* [PB13] or *iterative shrinkage-thresholding algorithm* [DDM04], where

$$\mathbf{x}^{(k+1)} = p_{f/L}\left(\mathbf{x}^{(k)} - \tfrac{1}{L}\nabla d\left(\mathbf{x}^{(k)}\right)\right) \,. \tag{2.18}$$

Here, L is a Lipschitz constant of ∇d, i.e., $\|\nabla d(\mathbf{x}_1) - \nabla d(\mathbf{x}_2)\| \leq L\,\|\mathbf{x}_1 - \mathbf{x}_2\|$ for all $\mathbf{x}_1$ and $\mathbf{x}_2$.

The algorithm in (2.18) converges with $\mathcal{O}(1/k)$. Its convergence can be improved by extrapolating from previous solutions. This leads to an *accelerated proximal gradient method*:

$$\hat{\mathbf{x}}^{(k+1)} = \mathbf{x}^{(k)} + \alpha^{(k)}(\mathbf{x}^{(k)} - \mathbf{x}^{(k-1)}) \,, \tag{2.19}$$

$$\mathbf{x}^{(k+1)} = p_{f/L}(\hat{\mathbf{x}}^{(k)} - \tfrac{1}{L}\nabla d(\hat{\mathbf{x}}^{(k)})) , \qquad (2.20)$$

with $0 \le \alpha^{(k)} < 1$. For an appropriate choice of $\alpha^{(k)}$, this converges with $\mathcal{O}(1/k^2)$. Examples are $\alpha^{(k)} = k/(k+3)$ [PB13] and $\alpha^{(k)} = \frac{t^{(k)}-1}{t^{(k+1)}}$ with $t^{(0)} = 1$ and $t^{(k+1)} = \frac{1+\sqrt{1+4t^{(k)^2}}}{2}$ [BT09]. The latter is known as the *fast iterative shrinkage-thresholding algorithm* (FISTA) and serves as the basis for the algorithms proposed in Chapters 4 to 6.

2.2.2 Lipschitz constant of the data term gradient

Proximal gradient methods require knowledge of the Lipschitz constant L of the data term $d(\mathbf{x})$. In the special case of (2.12), $d(\mathbf{x}) = \frac{1}{2}\|\mathbf{Mx} - \mathbf{y}\|_2^2$, so that $\nabla d = \mathbf{M}^\mathsf{T}(\mathbf{Mx} - \mathbf{y})$. Its Lipschitz constant L is then defined as

$$\left\|\mathbf{M}^\mathsf{T}\mathbf{M}(\mathbf{x}_1 - \mathbf{x}_2)\right\| \le L\left\|\mathbf{x}_1 - \mathbf{x}_2\right\| \qquad (2.21)$$

for all $\mathbf{x}_1$ and $\mathbf{x}_2$. The smallest such constant L is the largest eigenvalue $\lambda_{\max}$ of $\mathbf{M}^\mathsf{T}\mathbf{M}$. This can be seen by decomposing $\mathbf{M}$ and $\mathbf{x}_1 - \mathbf{x}_2$ in a basis $\mathbf{v}_i$ of eigenvectors of $\mathbf{M}$, such that $\mathbf{M}^\mathsf{T}\mathbf{M} = \sum_i \lambda_i \mathbf{v}_i \mathbf{v}_i^\mathsf{T}$ with $\|\mathbf{v}_i\| = 1$ and $\mathbf{v}_i^\mathsf{T}\mathbf{v}_j = \delta_{ij}$, and $\mathbf{x}_1 - \mathbf{x}_2 = \sum_i \alpha_i \mathbf{v}_i$. One can now rewrite the left-hand side of (2.21) as

$$\left\|\mathbf{M}^\mathsf{T}\mathbf{M}(\mathbf{x}_1 - \mathbf{x}_2)\right\| = \left\|\sum_i \lambda_i \mathbf{v}_i \mathbf{v}_i^\mathsf{T} \sum_j \alpha_j \mathbf{v}_j\right\| \qquad (2.22)$$

$$= \left\| \sum_i \lambda_i \alpha_i \mathbf{v}_i \right\| \tag{2.23}$$

$$\leq \lambda_{\max} \left\| \sum_i \alpha_i \mathbf{v}_i \right\| = L \left\| \mathbf{x}_1 - \mathbf{x}_2 \right\| , \tag{2.24}$$

proving the claim.

In practice, $\mathbf{M}$ and $\mathbf{M}^{\mathsf{T}}$ are often only defined by their product with a vector. This can provide enormous savings in memory and computation time. For example, in Chapter 6, the projection $\mathbf{P}$ of a volumetric grid into an image, $(\mathbf{Px})_{i,j} = \sum_k x_{i,j,k}$, can be computed efficiently without storing any matrix elements. Similarly, if $\mathbf{M}$ is a Fourier transform, as in Chapters 3 and 5, the Fast Fourier Transform algorithm [CT65] computes the matrix-vector product in $\mathcal{O}(n \log n)$ rather than $\mathcal{O}(n^2)$. The largest eigenvalue of such implicitly given $\mathbf{M}^{\mathsf{T}}\mathbf{M}$ can be computed using a *power iteration* scheme [TBI97, Algorithm 27.1]. Starting from a random vector $\mathbf{v}^{(0)}$,

$$\mathbf{v}^{(k+1)} = \frac{\mathbf{M}^{\mathsf{T}}\mathbf{M}\mathbf{v}^{(k)}}{\|\mathbf{M}^{\mathsf{T}}\mathbf{M}\mathbf{v}^{(k)}\|} \tag{2.25}$$

is iterated until convergence, and the magnitude of the largest eigenvalue is given as $\lambda = \|\mathbf{M}^{\mathsf{T}}\mathbf{M}\mathbf{v}\|$.

2.2.3 SpaRSA

Chapter 3 builds on the *sparse reconstruction by separable approximation* (SpaRSA) framework [WNF09]. It includes several different strategies for solving (2.12) and works well for complex data, like radio interferometric measurements. In each iteration of SpaRSA, a step size β is chosen and $\mathbf{x}^{(k+1)} = p_{\beta f}(\mathbf{x}^{(k)} - \beta \nabla d(\mathbf{x}^{(k)}))$ is computed. This is repeated for a sequence of exponentially shrinking β, until an *acceptance criterion* for β (and therefore $\mathbf{x}^{(k+1)}$) is fulfilled. Then, the subsequent $\mathbf{x}^{(k+2)}, \mathbf{x}^{(k+3)}, \ldots$ are computed in the same way until convergence is reached.

Different methods are proposed for choosing β and deciding acceptance. Two spectral methods for computing β make use of the difference between the last two iterates, $\mathbf{x}^{(k)} - \mathbf{x}^{(k-1)}$, so that

$$\beta = \frac{\left\| \mathbf{x}^{(k)} - \mathbf{x}^{(k-1)} \right\|_2^2}{\left\| \mathbf{M} \left(\mathbf{x}^{(k)} - \mathbf{x}^{(k-1)} \right) \right\|_2^2} \qquad (2.26)$$

or

$$\beta = \frac{\left\| \mathbf{M} \left(\mathbf{x}^{(k)} - \mathbf{x}^{(k-1)} \right) \right\|_2^2}{\left\| \mathbf{M}^\mathsf{T} \mathbf{M} \left(\mathbf{x}^{(k)} - \mathbf{x}^{(k-1)} \right) \right\|_2^2} . \qquad (2.27)$$

The most appropriate method depends on the problem type and the cost of evaluating matrix-vector products involving $\mathbf{M}$ and $\mathbf{M}^\mathsf{T}$.

The simplest acceptance criterion admits *any* choice of β. Alternatively, β is only accepted if it yields a sufficient decrease in the objective value when compared to the maximum objective value over the last few iterations, $\phi_{\max}$. Specifically, β is accepted if the objective is smaller than

$$\phi_{\max} - \frac{\sigma}{2\beta} \left\| \mathbf{x}^{(k)} - \mathbf{x}^{(k-1)} \right\|_2^2 \qquad (2.28)$$

for a given $\sigma \in (0, 1)$.

2.2.4 Other algorithms

Some further algorithms deserve to be mentioned here because they extend the range of solvable problems in interesting ways, although they are not put to use in the following chapters.

The *alternating direction method of multipliers* [BPC+11] provides an approach to solve (2.17) even for nondifferentiable d:

$$\mathbf{x}^{(k+1)} = p_{\beta d}(\mathbf{z}^{(k)} - \mathbf{u}^{(k)}) \qquad (2.29)$$

$$\mathbf{z}^{(k+1)} = p_{\beta f}(\mathbf{x}^{(k+1)} + \mathbf{u}^{(k)}) \qquad (2.30)$$

$$\mathbf{u}^{(k+1)} = \mathbf{u}^{(k)} + \mathbf{x}^{(k+1)} - \mathbf{z}^{(k+1)} . \qquad (2.31)$$

A similar primal–dual approach is given by [CP11].

Solving (2.12) for small λ often converges significantly more slowly than for larger values of λ. This makes it difficult to enforce the constraint $\mathbf{Mx} = \mathbf{y}$ exactly. Bregman iterations [GO09] provide a way to enforce exact constraints. They effectively solve

$$\arg\min_{\mathbf{x}} f(\mathbf{x}) \quad \text{subject to} \quad \mathbf{y} = \mathbf{Mx} \qquad (2.32)$$

by repeatedly applying

$$\mathbf{x}^{(k+1)} = \arg \min_{\mathbf{x}} \tfrac{1}{2} \left\| \mathbf{Mx} - \mathbf{y}^{(k)} \right\|_2^2 + \lambda f(\mathbf{x}) \qquad (2.33)$$

$$\mathbf{y}^{(k+1)} = \mathbf{y}^{(k)} + \mathbf{y} - \mathbf{Mx}^{(k)}, \qquad (2.34)$$

where f is convex. The regularization parameter λ does not need to be small, so that (2.33) can be solved efficiently using another proximal algorithm.

A completely different class of algorithms that does not rely on proximal mappings is tailored specifically to the problem of ℓ_1 minimization. This includes matching pursuit [MZ93], orthogonal matching pursuit [TG07], regularized orthogonal matching pursuit [NV09], and hard thresholding pursuit [Fou11]. However, because of their lower flexibility compared to proximal algorithms, they will not be used in the following and are only listed here for completeness.

2.2.5 General techniques

Some general techniques apply to SpaRSA and FISTA as well as related iterative algorithms. Good overviews are found in [FNW07; WNF09], from which the following ideas are taken.

For any iterative algorithm, a criterion is necessary to decide when to stop iterating. The most basic approach is to stop after a fixed number of steps. It is also common to stop iterating when the relative change in $\mathbf{x}^{(k)}$ or the relative change in the objective function value

drop below a specified threshold. However, in some algorithms, intermediate solutions stay almost constant for several iterations before
convergence is reached, or the objective function value even grows over
a few iterations; in these cases, the stopping criterion must typically
be satisfied for several subsequent iterations before the iteration is
actually stopped. More complex stopping criteria involve known upper
bounds of either the distance between the intermediate solution and
the minimizer (using a linear complementary problem, or LCP), or
the difference between the objective function value and the minimum
(based on the *duality gap*, the difference to the maximum of the dual
problem). To evaluate the performance of an algorithm, very simple
stopping criteria are often sufficient; in the following chapters, the
algorithm is, in general, terminated after a fixed number of steps.

In general, proximal algorithms converge slowly for small λ, but
benefit from a good initial guess for $\mathbf{x}$. It therefore often makes
sense to *warm start* the algorithm with a solution for slightly larger
λ. This leads to so-called *continuation schemes*, where a decreasing
sequence of $\lambda^{(k)}$ is chosen and reconstructions are run for each $\lambda^{(k)}$,
initializing $\mathbf{x}$ with the result of the previous run. An example [WNF09]
is $\lambda^{(k+1)} \propto \lambda_{\max}(\mathbf{M}, \mathbf{y} - \mathbf{M}\mathbf{x}^{(k)})$, where $\mathbf{x}^{(k)}$ is the result of the previous
run, and $\lambda_{\max}(\mathbf{M}, \mathbf{y})$ is the smallest λ such that the solution of (2.12)
is the zero vector.

For any $\lambda > 0$, the constraint $\mathbf{M}\mathbf{x} = \mathbf{y}$ will only approximately be
fulfilled. If the regularization term is only meant to induce sparsity,

this is an unwanted bias. An additional *debiasing* step can be used to maintain good compliance with the constraints once a sparse solution is found. A straightforward approach is keeping the sparsity pattern fixed and then minimizing $\|\mathbf{Mx} - \mathbf{y}\|_2^2$ by varying only the nonzero entries of $\mathbf{x}$.

2.3 Regularizers and proximal mappings

For the performance of any proximal algorithm, it is crucial that the proximal mapping p_f can be evaluated efficiently. In general, this may require a sub-algorithm to iteratively approximate (2.16). However, there are a few important cases where more efficient algorithms or even closed-form solutions exist.

2.3.1 ℓ_1-norm

An especially efficient method exists to compute the proximal mapping of the ℓ_1-norm,

$$p_{\beta\|\cdot\|_1}(\mathbf{x}) = \arg\min_{\mathbf{w}} \tfrac{1}{2} \|\mathbf{w} - \mathbf{x}\|_2^2 + \beta \|\mathbf{w}\|_1 \ , \qquad (2.35)$$

which is used in Chapters 3 and 4. To derive the solution, the concept of the gradient of a function has to be generalized to nondifferentiable functions. This is achieved by defining the *subgradient* of a convex function $f : \mathbb{R}^n \to \mathbb{R}$ as

$$\partial f(\mathbf{x}) = \left\{ \mathbf{v} \in \mathbb{R}^n \; \middle| \; f(\bar{\mathbf{x}}) - f(\mathbf{x}) \geq \mathbf{v}^\mathsf{T}(\bar{\mathbf{x}} - \mathbf{x}) \quad \forall \bar{\mathbf{x}} \in \mathbb{R}^n \right\} . \quad (2.36)$$

It can be interpreted as the set of gradient vectors of all tangent hyperplanes to f in $\mathbf{x}$.

The necessary condition for optimality of (2.35) can now be written

$$0 \in \partial \left(\tfrac{1}{2} \left\| \mathbf{w} - \mathbf{x} \right\|_2^2 + \beta \left\| \mathbf{w} \right\|_1 \right) = \mathbf{w} - \mathbf{x} + \beta \partial \left\| \mathbf{w} \right\|_1 , \quad (2.37)$$

where ∂ operates with respect to $\mathbf{w}$. Since this is separable in the components of $\mathbf{w}$, the components w_i can be considered separately,

$$0 \in w_i - x_i + \beta \partial |w_i| . \quad (2.38)$$

For $w_i \neq 0$, $|w_i|$ is differentiable, and $\partial |w_i| = \operatorname{sgn} w_i$, so that (2.38) becomes

$$0 = w_i - x_i + \beta \operatorname{sgn} w_i . \quad (2.39)$$

If the optimal w_i is negative, $\operatorname{sgn} w_i = -1$, and $x_i + \beta = w_i < 0$, i.e., $x_i < -\beta$. On the other hand, if w_i is positive, $\operatorname{sgn} w_i = 1$, and $x_i - \beta = w_i > 0$, i.e., $x_i > \beta$. In summary, $w_i \neq 0$ results in $|x_i| > \beta$ and $\operatorname{sgn} x_i = \operatorname{sgn} w_i$, so that (2.39) becomes

$$w_i = x_i - \beta \operatorname{sgn} x_i = (|x_i| - \beta) \operatorname{sgn} x_i . \quad (2.40)$$

For the case of $w_i = 0$, $\partial |w_i|$ is the interval $[-1, 1]$, and (2.38) becomes $0 \in -x_i + \beta[-1, 1]$, i.e., $|x_i| \leq \beta$.

The above solutions, $w_i = (|x_i| - \beta)\operatorname{sgn} x_i$ for $|x_i| > \beta$ and $w_i = 0$ for $|x_i| <= \beta$, can be conveniently summarized as

$$w_i = \max\left(|x_i| - \beta, 0\right)\operatorname{sgn} x_i .\tag{2.41}$$

This expression is referred to as the *soft thresholding operator*. In vectorial form, it defines the proximal mapping of the ℓ_1-norm,

$$p_{\beta\|\cdot\|_1}(\mathbf{x}) = \max(|\mathbf{x}| - \beta, 0)\operatorname{sgn}\mathbf{x} .\tag{2.42}$$

For complex $\mathbf{x}$, $|\mathbf{x}|$ is replaced by the magnitude of the components of $\mathbf{x}$, and the complex phase angle takes the place of the signum function. This can be considered a special case of $\ell_{1,2}$ minimization, which is discussed in Section 2.3.4.

In many applications, the components of $\mathbf{x}$ are known to be non-negative. For example, the radio flux densities in Chapters 3 and 5 and the volumetric emission in Chapters 4 and 6 represent physical quantities that are always positive. This can be enforced by setting

$$f(\mathbf{x}) = \|\mathbf{x}\|_1 + I^+(\mathbf{x}) ,\tag{2.43}$$

where the indicator function $I^+(\mathbf{x})$ is 0 if all $x_i \geq 0$, and ∞ otherwise. The corresponding proximal mapping is

$$p^+_{\beta\|\cdot\|_1}(\mathbf{x}) = \max(\mathbf{x} - \beta, 0) .\tag{2.44}$$

2.3.2 Dual norms

Chapters 5 and 6 are based on minimization of the ℓ_∞-norm. The proximal mapping of this norm can be derived from a more general statement about the proximal mappings of *dual norms*. If f is a *norm*, $f = \|\cdot\|$, then its proximal mapping can be written as an optimization problem [PB13, section 2.5]

$$p_{\beta f}(\mathbf{x}) = \mathbf{x} - \arg\min_{\mathbf{w}} \|\mathbf{w} - \mathbf{x}\|_2^2 \quad \text{s.t.} \quad \|\mathbf{w}\|_* \leq \beta , \qquad (2.45)$$

that is constrained by the corresponding dual norm

$$\|\mathbf{w}\|_* = \sup \left\{ \mathbf{w}^\mathsf{T}\mathbf{x} \,\middle|\, \|\mathbf{x}\| \leq 1 \right\} . \qquad (2.46)$$

Graphically speaking, the constrained optimization problem (2.45) describes an orthogonal projection of $\mathbf{x}$ onto the $\|\cdot\|_*$-ball of radius β.

To derive (2.45), the convex conjugate of f is defined as

$$f^*(\mathbf{w}) = \sup_{\mathbf{x}}(\mathbf{w}^\mathsf{T}\mathbf{x} - f(\mathbf{x})) = \sup_{\mathbf{x}}(\mathbf{w}^\mathsf{T}\mathbf{x} - \|\mathbf{x}\|) . \qquad (2.47)$$

If there is any $\mathbf{x}$ for which $\mathbf{w}^\mathsf{T}\mathbf{x} - \|\mathbf{x}\| > 0$, then $f^*(\mathbf{w}) = \infty$ (via homogeneity of $\|\cdot\|$); otherwise, $f^*(\mathbf{w}) = 0$ (e.g., for $\mathbf{x} = 0$). Such an $\mathbf{x}$ exists if and only if $\|\mathbf{w}\|_* = \sup \left\{ \mathbf{w}^\mathsf{T}\mathbf{x} \,\middle|\, \|\mathbf{x}\| \leq 1 \right\} > 1$. Thus, $f^*(\mathbf{w}) = 0$ for $\|\mathbf{w}\|_* \leq 1$, and ∞ otherwise; f^* is an *indicator function* for the $\|\cdot\|_*$-unit ball. (2.45) now follows from the *Moreau decomposition* [PB13]

$$\mathbf{x} = p_{\beta f}(\mathbf{x}) + \beta p_{f^*/\beta}(\mathbf{x}/\beta) \qquad (2.48)$$

by noting that the proximal mapping p_{f^*} is the orthogonal projection onto the $\|\cdot\|_*$-unit ball, and $\beta p_{f^*/\beta}(\mathbf{x}/\beta)$ is the projection onto the $\|\cdot\|_*$-ball with radius β.

2.3.3 ℓ_∞-norm

It is easy to see from (2.46) that the dual of the ℓ_∞-norm, which is used in Chapters 5 and 6, is the ℓ_1-norm. This means that the proximal mapping for the ℓ_∞-norm can be directly computed from a projection of $\mathbf{x}$ onto an ℓ_1-ball with radius β. Unfortunately, this projection is not trivial to compute.

A straightforward solution is to truncate all components that currently share the largest absolute value until they reach the second largest (or the ℓ_1-norm of the residual is equal to β), and to repeat the process until the ℓ_1-norm of the residual is equal to β. By presorting the components according to their magnitude, $\mathcal{O}(n \log n)$ complexity can be achieved [DFL08]. This can be further improved by using a heap structure to access the components in order of decreasing absolute value without necessarily sorting the whole vector [BF08].

A probabilistic approach [DSSSC08] is able to compute the projection on the ℓ_1-ball in $\mathcal{O}(n)$ expected time by repeatedly partitioning the components of $|\mathbf{x}|$ with respect to a random pivot element. If the sum of the differences between the pivot and the larger elements exceeds $\|\mathbf{x}\|_1 - \beta$, the smaller elements can be excluded from further processing; otherwise, all larger elements are known to change, and further processing can continue with the smaller elements only, keeping track of the accumulated "large" elements.

In all algorithms, an early exit is possible if $\|\mathbf{x}\|_1 \leq \beta$, and the implementation is simplified by working with $|\mathbf{x}|$ and subsequently reconstructing the signs.

Since the physical quantities in Chapters 5 and 6 are known to be nonnegative, it is desirable to include this a priori knowledge in the regularization term. The proximal mapping for the ℓ_∞-norm with such a nonnegativity constraint can be computed by simply thresholding $\mathbf{x}$ before applying the proximal mapping,

$$p^+_{\beta\|\cdot\|_\infty}(\mathbf{x}) = p_{\beta\|\cdot\|_\infty}(\max(\mathbf{x}, 0)) . \tag{2.49}$$

This can be seen as follows: the convex conjugate of $f(\mathbf{x}) = \beta \|\mathbf{x}\|_\infty + I^+(\mathbf{x})$, where $I^+(\mathbf{x})$ is 0 if all $x_i \geq 0$ and ∞ otherwise, is

$$f^*(\mathbf{x}^*) = \sup_{\mathbf{x}} \langle \mathbf{x}^*, \mathbf{x} \rangle - \beta \|\mathbf{x}\|_\infty - I^+(\mathbf{x}) \tag{2.50}$$

$$= \sup_{\mathbf{x}} \sum_i x_i^* x_i - \beta \max \mathbf{x} \quad \text{s.t.} \quad \mathbf{x} \geq 0 \tag{2.51}$$

$$= \sup_{\mathbf{x}} (\sum_{x_i^* > 0} x_i^* - \beta) \max \mathbf{x} \quad \text{s.t.} \quad \mathbf{x} \geq 0 \tag{2.52}$$

$$= \begin{cases} 0 & \text{if } \sum_{x_i^* > 0} x_i^* \leq \beta \\ \infty & \text{otherwise} \end{cases} \qquad (2.53)$$

Therefore, $p_{f^*}(\mathbf{x})$ is the orthogonal projection onto $\sum_{x_i > 0} x_i \leq \beta$, an ℓ_1-ball with radius β. For the vector $\mathbf{x}^+$ consisting only of the positive components of $\mathbf{x}$, this means that $p_{\beta\|\cdot\|_\infty}^+(\mathbf{x}^+) = p_f(\mathbf{x}^+) = p_{\beta\|\cdot\|_\infty}(\mathbf{x}^+)$. For the vector $\mathbf{x}^-$ consisting of the nonpositive components, on the other hand, $p_{f^*}(\mathbf{x}^-)$ is the identity, so that $p_{\beta\|\cdot\|_\infty}^+(\mathbf{x}^-) = \mathbf{x}^- - p_{f^*}(\mathbf{x}^-)$ is zero. Since additional zero components in $\mathbf{x}$ do not influence $p_{\beta\|\cdot\|_\infty}(\mathbf{x})$, one can equivalently threshold negative entries of $\mathbf{x}$ to zero and then apply $p_{\beta\|\cdot\|_\infty}$, proving the claim.

2.3.4 Separable regularizers

The group sparsity methods presented in Chapters 5 and 6 require the computation of proximal mappings for certain regularizers f that separable, such that $f(\mathbf{x}) = \sum_{g \in G} f_g(\mathbf{x}_{[g]})$ (2.13). In this case, the proximal mappings for the f_g can be applied to each $\mathbf{x}_{[g]}$ individually [FR08; WNF09]. Such separable regularizers are often used to achieve *joint sparsity* of signal components. Since norms are nonnegative, a separable regularizer with $f_g = \|\cdot\|_p$ can be interpreted as the ℓ_1-norm of the vector consisting of the ℓ_p-norms of the groups g; this is often called an $\ell_{1,p}$-norm. Popular choices for group sparsity regularizers are $\ell_{1,2}$-norms and $\ell_{1,\infty}$-norms. $\ell_{1,2}$-norms can be used, for example, to achieve ℓ_1 regularization of a complex signal without affecting the phase angle (cf. Section 2.3.1). $\ell_{1,\infty}$-norms, on the other hand, favor uniform distribution of energy within a group.

2.3.5 Relation to probability distributions

The effect of a certain class of regularizers, the pth power of an ℓ_p-norm, $f(\mathbf{x}) = \|\mathbf{x}\|_p^p$, can be interpreted in the context of Bayesian statistics. This includes the ℓ_1-norm, which will frequently be used in the following chapters. Regularization with such f can be interpreted as maximum a posteriori estimation assuming a generalized Gaussian probability distribution $\mathcal{P}(x_i) = \exp(-|x_i|^p)$ for the components of $\mathbf{x}$ [CCPW07, section 4]. These regularizers are separable, so that the proximal mapping can be computed independently for the components. Closed form solutions for $p \in \{1, 4/3, 3/2, 2, 3, 4\}$ exist; for other p, solutions can often be obtained iteratively using the Newton method. The special case of $p = 2$ is also known as Tikhonov regularization [Vog02]. Related optimization approaches with probabilistic interpretation include the maximum likelihood [SD04] and maximization entropy methods [CE85; SB84].

3 Sparsity Reconstruction

The theory of compressed sensing has a natural application in interferometric aperture synthesis [PSB89]. In an interferometric radio telescope, Figure 3.1(a), information about radio emission from a small region of the sky, Figure 3.1(b), is obtained in the form of samples in the Fourier transform domain of the sky image. The correlations between the signals from multiple antennas yield information about the spatial frequency content of the image, eventually allowing the image itself to be reconstructed. Since the size of the synthesized beam of such a telescope is inversely proportional to the largest distance between any two antennas, very high spatial resolutions can be obtained this way. However, the process of reconstructing the image from incomplete frequency information is highly nontrivial, as missing information has to be appropriately reconstructed.

In this chapter, a sparsity-based method for solving the interferometric reconstruction problem is developed. Since compressed sensing theory does not make any propositions about the non-random Fourier domain sampling appearing in interferometry, a numerical experiment

(a) The Very Large Array.   (b) Centaurus A.

Figure 3.1: Radio interferometers like the VLA (a) indirectly capture images of the sky at radio wavelengths. In the radio galaxy Centaurus A (b), the lobes of a jet can be discerned in the radio wavelengths (colored) but not in the visible spectrum.

is performed first to investigate the influence of non-random sampling on reconstruction quality. The method is then evaluated quantitatively on realistic simulations, and qualitatively on actual radio interferometric measurements.

3.1 Background

Since the middle of the twentieth century, interferometric techniques have been used to obtain images of the sky at radio wavelengths [PSB89; RH60; RV46; SJM68]. Modern radio telescope arrays consist of several antennas that pick up electromagnetic waves from astronomical sources. The source distribution can be described by the electric amplitude

$A(\mathbf{k})$ originating from direction $\mathbf{k}$. For distant sources, the propagation can be approximated by a plane wave, where $\mathbf{k}$ is the wave vector (the direction scaled to length $2\pi/\lambda$, with wavelength λ). After applying a band-pass filter to select the desired radio frequency $\omega/2\pi$, the electric field strength $E(\mathbf{r})$ at antenna location $\mathbf{r}$ can be written as

$$E(\mathbf{r}) = \int A(\mathbf{k}) e^{i(\mathbf{kr} - \omega t + \phi(\mathbf{k},t))} \, d\Omega \,, \tag{3.1}$$

where integration is over all directions $\mathbf{k}$ with $\|\mathbf{k}\| = \omega/c_0$, and c_0 is the speed of light. $\phi(\mathbf{k}, t)$ is the phase of the wave from direction $\mathbf{k}$, which may change randomly over time t. The time-averaged correlation between antennas at $\mathbf{r}_i$ and $\mathbf{r}_j$ is then

$$V(\mathbf{r}_i - \mathbf{r}_j) = \langle E(\mathbf{r}_i) E^*(\mathbf{r}_j) \rangle \tag{3.2}$$

$$= \frac{1}{T} \int_0^T \iint A(\mathbf{k}_i) A(\mathbf{k}_j) e^{i(\mathbf{k}_i \mathbf{r}_i - \mathbf{k}_j \mathbf{r}_j)}$$

$$\cdot e^{i(\phi(\mathbf{k}_i,t) - \phi(\mathbf{k}_j,t))} \, d\Omega_i \, d\Omega_j \, dt \tag{3.3}$$

$$= \int I(\mathbf{k}) e^{i\mathbf{k}(\mathbf{r}_i - \mathbf{r}_j)} \, d\Omega \,. \tag{3.4}$$

The last step is based on the assumption that radiation from different points on the sky is uncorrelated, so that $\phi(\mathbf{k}_i, t) - \phi(\mathbf{k}_j, t)$ is random for $i \neq j$, and therefore causes terms with $\mathbf{k}_i \neq \mathbf{k}_j$ to average out over time. In addition, the squared amplitude is replaced by the incident energy $I(\mathbf{k}) = A(\mathbf{k})^2$.

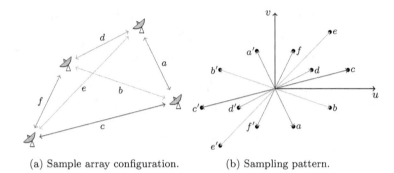

(a) Sample array configuration. (b) Sampling pattern.

Figure 3.2: Hypothetical interferometric array configuration (a) and resulting sampling pattern in the frequency domain (b). Each vectorial distance between any pair of antennas corresponds to the location of one sample point. One array configuration and sampling pattern for the VLA telescope are shown in Figures 3.3(a) and 3.3(c), respectively.

The correlation $V(\mathbf{r}_i - \mathbf{r}_j)$ of the signals from two antennas is called *visibility*. Each visibility corresponds to a single complex entry in the Fourier transform of the image I. The location of this entry in the transform domain is determined by the distance vector between both antennas, the *baseline* $\mathbf{r}_i - \mathbf{r}_j$, Figure 3.2.

Under the assumption that the sources being imaged are confined to a small region of the sky, $\mathbf{k}$ can be discretized on a plane such that $\mathbf{k} \approx (i, j, 1)^{\mathsf{T}}$. Writing $\mathbf{r}_i - \mathbf{r}_j = (u, v, w)^{\mathsf{T}}$, this corresponds to a two-dimensional Fourier transform multiplied by a phase, such that

$$y_{u,v,w} \approx \mathrm{e}^{\mathrm{i}w} \sum_{i,j} x_{i,j} \mathrm{e}^{\mathrm{i}(iu+jv)} \,, \tag{3.5}$$

where $\mathbf{x}$ and $\mathbf{y}$ are the discretized image I and visibilities V, respectively.

3.2 Related work

Obtaining the sky image from measured visibilities is an ill-posed inverse problem, and several approaches have been used to solve it. Traditionally, the iterative deconvolution algorithm CLEAN [Hög74], essentially a matching pursuit algorithm [LAM97], is used for the reconstruction of radio interferometric images in radio interferometry software like AIPS [Aip] and CASA [Cas]. CLEAN is a greedy algorithm that implicitly assumes that the image is composed of a small number of point sources. It starts from the *dirty image*, a minimum energy reconstruction obtained by *gridding* the visibilities onto a regular grid and applying the inverse Fast Fourier Transform (FFT). It then successively subtracts a user-defined fraction of the *point spread function* (PSF, the Fourier transform of the sampling pattern) around the brightest spots of the image and records the position and amount of subtracted intensity. Finally, the map of recorded positions is convolved with the *clean beam*, representing the supposed best possible resolution, which is determined from the main lobe of the PSF.

This process works well for images of isolated point sources, but does not always produce satisfying results for extended sources. Also, the convergence of the algorithm as well as the uniqueness of its solutions are not always guaranteed [Sch78; Sch79]. Regions that are supposed to be dark in the image are often manually excluded from the reconstruction process in order to avoid artifacts in these regions, reducing reproducibility. Modifications to the algorithm have been proposed that try to reduce this and other objectionable effects [Cor83; Sch84; SF78] or aim for better reconstructions of extended sources using a multi-scale approach [Cor08]. Related reconstruction algorithms used in the context of radio interferometry include the maximum entropy method [CE85], analysis by synthesis [DMF12], and Bayesian inference [SWM+14].

Even though many improvements to CLEAN have been proposed, extended intensity distributions are still not always well reconstructed, and the process may require considerable user guidance in order to yield satisfactory results. Besides, new telescopes like the Long Wavelength Array LWA [ECC+09], the Low Frequency Array LOFAR [VGN09] or the Square Kilometre Array SKA [Eke03; Sch04] that image large parts of the sky at once require reconstruction algorithms that handle increasing amounts of data as well as non-coplanar telescope and image geometries [CGB08; MS08]. Also, with a growing amount of available data sets, a more automatic reconstruction pipeline is desirable.

Compressed sensing allows for a mathematically sound formulation of an important class of algorithms based on maximization of a plausibility function. Some compressed sensing algorithms have successfully been applied to astronomy [BSO08], including radio interferometry. In previous work [WJP+09; WPV10], basis pursuit algorithms were used to recover simulated images of different radio sources (random Gaussians and string signals) from *simulated measurements* as a proof of concept. [Suk09] applied similar methods to real observational data from the Very Large Array (VLA), using total variation minimization for regularization. However, the exact solver employed there is not suitable for large-scale problems.

In contrast, the algorithm presented in the following section can be shown to work with data from real radio interferometers and permits a wide choice of different regularizers in order to reconstruct a wide range of sources. Results similar to those of CLEAN can be obtained by using the ℓ_1-norm of the image pixels as a regularizer. It is also stable with respect to the errors introduced by the physical measurement process [Zhu08], and, as an approximate solver, is more efficient than convex optimization codes used for basis pursuit, especially for high-dimensional problems.

3.3 Algorithm

The method presented in this chapter is based on SpaRSA (cf. Section 2.2.3) with an adaptive continuation scheme (cf. Section 2.2.5). It computes a solution to

$$\arg\min_{\mathbf{x}} f(\mathbf{x}) \quad \text{subject to} \quad \|\mathbf{Mx} - \mathbf{y}\|_2^2 \le \|\sigma\|^2 , \qquad (3.6)$$

where $f(\mathbf{x})$ is the ℓ_1-norm of $\mathbf{x}$ in an appropriate basis (cf. Section 3.4), by repeatedly solving

$$\arg\min_{\mathbf{x}} \tfrac{1}{2} \|\mathbf{Mx} - \mathbf{y}\|_2^2 + \lambda f(\mathbf{x}) \qquad (2.12)$$

for a decreasing sequence of λ. The expected noise level σ can be derived from several known or measured parameters of the observation, such as the temperature of the antenna or the duration of the measurement.

Pseudocode for the method is given in Algorithm 1. The solution vector $\mathbf{x}$ is initialized as the dirty image, $\mathbf{M}^T\mathbf{y}$. The outer loop of the continuation scheme computes λ from the residual $\mathbf{Mx} - \mathbf{y}$ as proposed in [WNF09, section III], and (2.12) is solved in an inner loop. The step size β is computed by a simple spectral method. The inner loop exits as soon as the absolute change in the objective function value drops below a specified threshold (here, $\epsilon = 10^{-6}$). If the new residual is still above the noise level, λ is recomputed and another iteration

---

Algorithm 1 Modified SpaRSA algorithm for minimizing $f(\mathbf{x})$ subject to $\|\mathbf{Mx} - \mathbf{y}\|_2^2 \leq \|\sigma\|^2$.

$\mathbf{x}^{(0)} \leftarrow \mathbf{M}^\mathsf{T}\mathbf{y}$, $\beta^{(0)} \leftarrow 1$, $k \leftarrow 1$

repeat

$\qquad \lambda \leftarrow \left\| \mathbf{M}^\mathsf{T}(\mathbf{Mx}^{(k-1)} - \mathbf{y}) \right\|_\infty$

$\qquad$ **repeat**

$\qquad\qquad \mathbf{x}^{(k)} \leftarrow p_{\beta\lambda f}(\mathbf{x}^{(k-1)} - \beta\mathbf{M}^\mathsf{T}(\mathbf{Mx}^{(k-1)} - \mathbf{y}))$

$\qquad\qquad \beta \leftarrow \dfrac{\left\|\mathbf{x}^{(k)}-\mathbf{x}^{(k-1)}\right\|_2^2}{\left\|\mathbf{M}(\mathbf{x}^{(k)}-\mathbf{x}^{(k-1)})\right\|_2^2}$

$\qquad\qquad k \leftarrow k+1$

$\qquad$ **until** change in $\frac{1}{2}\left\|\mathbf{Mx}^{(k)} - \mathbf{y}\right\|_2^2 + \lambda f(\mathbf{x}^{(k)}) \leq \epsilon$

until $\left\|\mathbf{Mx}^{(k)} - \mathbf{y}\right\|_2 \leq \|\sigma\|_2$

---

is started from the intermediate result until the residual eventually fulfills the constraint of (3.6).

For efficiency reasons, matrix products with $\mathbf{M}$ and $\mathbf{M}^\mathsf{T}$ are implemented as two-dimensional forward and backward FFT, respectively. Since, in practice, the visibilities do not lie on a regular grid (as required by the FFT), gridding is necessary. This inevitably introduces slight quantization errors; a method to minimize these errors is presented in Chapter 5.

3.4 Sparsity priors

The selection of a sparsity basis or *sparsity prior* represents the assumptions made about the image and as such can strongly influence the reconstruction. For example, sparsity in the pixel basis is well suited to represent the assumption of isolated point sources, and is implicitly used in the conventional CLEAN algorithm. In contrast, most terrestrial images are likely to contain large regions of homogeneous or slowly changing intensity, possibly with small-scale perturbations or sharp edges. For this case, appropriate sparsity bases are known that can also be used for astronomical imaging. For example, different wavelet representations [CDF92; Dau88] efficiently compress many natural images because they provide a scaling-independent but localized basis. In the following, the ℓ_1-norm in the pixel basis or in a wavelet basis will be used as a regularizer as indicated.

3.5 The role of randomness

Radio interferometry, like many other real-world applications, violates the assumption of truly random sampling which is elementary to many propositions of compressed sensing. The possibility of perfect reconstruction from Fourier measurements is only proven for random sampling of the frequencies (cf. Section 2.1.4), but the sampling patterns induced by an interferometric array configuration exhibit a large degree of regularity, Figure 3.3. In fact, the positions of all $n(n-1)$ samples are uniquely defined by only n sensor positions, Figure 3.2. Truly random sample distributions cannot be obtained because the sampling is constrained by the measurement process. In addition, the resulting patterns are naturally biased towards low frequencies, Figure 3.3(c).

On the other hand, many real-world applications rely on similar non-random sampling in the frequency domain, and compressed sensing has been successfully applied to some of these problems. For the case of magnetic resonance imaging (MRI), several types of non-random frequency sampling have been compared [LDP07]. Another classical example is the successful reconstruction of a piecewise constant signal from simulated tomography measurements where the frequency sampling pattern consists of radial lines; nevertheless, pathological cases exist where regular sampling of the Fourier domain makes reconstruction impossible [CRT06a]. While applications of compressed sensing to interferometry have been proposed before [WJP+09; WPV10], these works neither investigate the influence of non-random sampling, nor is the reconstruction algorithm validated on observational data.

3.5.1 Numerical experiment

In order to evaluate the influence of random sampling on reconstruction quality, sampling patterns that are generated from real or hypothetical sensor positions are compared to randomly generated patterns. Figure 3.3(a) shows the sensor positions for the VLA telescope; the corresponding sampling pattern is displayed in Figure 3.3(c). From the actual sampling pattern, a randomized pattern is generated, Fig-

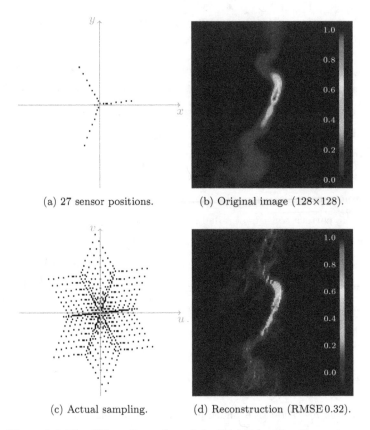

(a) 27 sensor positions.   (b) Original image (128×128).

(c) Actual sampling.   (d) Reconstruction (RMSE 0.32).

Figure 3.3: The 'D' configuration of the VLA telescope, i.e., antenna positions in world coordinates (a) and the corresponding sampling pattern in the frequency domain (c). A radio map of the radio galaxy 3C31 (b) was reconstructed from simulated measurements by minimizing the ℓ_1-norm in the pixel basis (d).

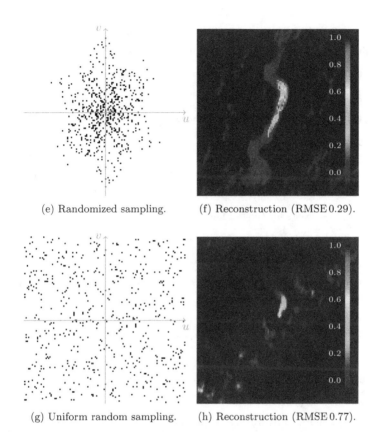

(e) Randomized sampling.

(f) Reconstruction (RMSE 0.29).

(g) Uniform random sampling.

(h) Reconstruction (RMSE 0.77).

Figure 3.3 (continued): A randomized sampling pattern (e) with the same large-scale distribution and number of samples as (c), and a uniform random sampling pattern (g). Note that neither sampling pattern can be realized by a physical sensor configuration. Corresponding reconstructions are shown in (f) and (h), respectively.

ure 3.3(e). It inherits the large-scale frequency distribution, the number of samples, and the point symmetry of the actual pattern, but does not exhibit the regularity of a pattern produced by any possible configuration of antenna positions. Finally, another point symmetric pattern with uniformly random sample distribution is generated for comparison, Figure 3.3(g).

Based on these patterns, measurements are simulated on a radio image of the galaxy 3C31, Figure 3.3(b). Since no possible telescope configuration exists for the random patterns, the simulated measurements cannot be obtained from the simulation of a physical measurement device. Instead, the measurement matrix is directly applied to the ground truth image to obtain the measurement vector. More realistic simulations are covered in Section 3.6.1.

After computing the simulated measurement vector from the ground truth image, reconstructions are performed using the proposed CS algorithm. The reconstruction results from actual, Figure 3.3(d), and randomized patterns, Figure 3.3(f), both provide much better visual reconstruction quality and lower root mean squared error (RMSE) than the reconstruction from a uniformly, randomly sampled Fourier domain, Figure 3.3(h). This observation implies that the emphasis on low frequencies induced by actual sampling is more important to reconstruction quality than randomness of the sampling. This can be explained by the higher energy content of low frequencies in natural images which overcompensates for the fact that some high-frequency regions are not sampled at all by actual interferometric array patterns.

3.5.2 Statistical evaluation

Based on this initial result, the influence of non-random and non-uniform sampling is further investigated for a wide range of parameters. For different numbers of sensors, sensor positions are chosen at random, and the resulting sampling pattern is computed. Subsequently, randomized and uniformly random patterns are generated as described earlier. For each number of sensors, 28 such configurations are generated, measurements of the source image are simulated, and the image is reconstructed. The resulting RMSE values are shown in Figure 3.4.

The result of the statistical evaluation largely supports the hypothesis that radiointerferometric sampling patterns allow for similar reconstruction quality as the completely random patterns for which compressed sensing theory proves optimality. Over the entire parameter range, randomized sampling differs only minimally from actual sampling, while uniformly random sampling requires more samples to attain comparable RMSE. As the number of samples approaches the number of pixels in the image, all kinds of sampling contain enough information to reconstruct the image almost perfectly, in accordance with compressed sensing theory.

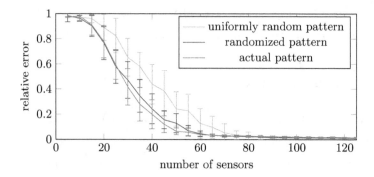

Figure 3.4: Mean normalized RMSE of reconstruction results from simulated measurements. For each number of sensors, 28 sampling patterns were generated from random sensor positions (red). From each sampling, random patterns with the same large-scale distribution and number of sampling points were created (green). For comparison, patterns with uniform random sample distribution were used (blue). The error bars indicate one standard deviation. Note that the reconstruction quality for "actual" (physically realizable) antenna distributions and randomized sampling patterns with the same density distribution does not differ significantly, while completely random sampling produces distinctly worse results.

This statistical evaluation of the influence of different sampling patterns on reconstruction quality shows that the kind of non-random sampling that occurs in interferometric measurements does not introduce noticeable deteriorating effects. Instead, the natural emphasis on low frequencies in realistic sampling increases reconstruction quality for natural images, and astronomical objects with similar image statistics, when compared to uniformly random patterns.

As the kind of non-random sampling that occurs in radio interferometric imaging does not seem to impair the quality of image reconstruction, the proposed method can be expected to reach the full performance of compressed sensing when applied to such measurements.

3.6 Results

The performance of the proposed approach is evaluated and compared to traditional methods using different datasets, two synthetic ones and two from the Very Large Array.

3.6.1 Simulated data

For a synthetic source, the 'ground truth' image is known, allowing for objective performance comparison of different reconstruction algorithms. In contrast to Section 3.5.1, the measurements used for this experiment were simulated using the CASA `simdata` task, which emulates several realistic sources of error, including gridding. Three different error metrics are evaluated:

- the signal-to-noise ratio $\text{SNR} = 20\,\text{dB}\cdot\log_{10}\frac{\sigma}{\sigma_r}$ [WJP+09], where σ and σ_r are the standard deviations of the original image and of its difference to the reconstruction, respectively;

- the RMSE normalized to the average of the true image; and

- the dynamic range, defined as the ratio of the highest peak in the reconstruction to the standard deviation of the reconstruction noise measured in supposedly empty regions of the image.

The dynamic range is a common no-reference error metric in radio interferometry; however, its significance in this setting is rather limited because of the nonlinearity of the algorithms.

Figure 3.5(a) shows two simulated sources that are reasonably similar to real, extended radio sources: a uniform gradient with Gaussian decay and a series of Gaussians of increasing size. The large regions of extended emission, together with comparatively low sampling density, deliberately push the algorithms to their limits so that the differences in reconstruction quality become visible. The UV coverage—i.e., the fraction of grid cells for which visibility data is known after gridding at the specified image resolution, in this case 256×256 pixels—is 4.2% from a simulated 6000 s VLA observation in the 'D' configuration. Each pixel in the simulated image corresponds to one arcsecond, and the CLEAN beam has a full width at half maximum (FWHM) of $7.4'' \times 4.7''$.

For reference, CLEAN reconstructions (b) were made using the implementation from the CASA software package [Cla80]. In order to make the results user-independent and comparable, both reconstruction algorithms were run with their default parameters (for CLEAN, these

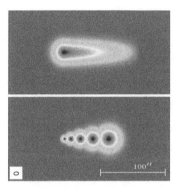

(a) Synthetic sources.

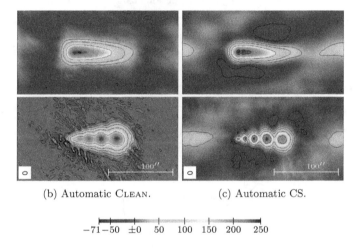

(b) Automatic CLEAN. (c) Automatic CS.

Figure 3.5: Measurements of synthetic sources (a) were simulated and reconstructions were performed using CLEAN with the default parameters (b) and Daubechies wavelet ℓ_1 minimization (c). Contour levels are plotted—except for the noise-free originals—at $-1, 1, 2, 4, \ldots, 2^n$ times the respective 3σ RMS noise. All images are 256×256 pixels ($256'' \times 256''$), and the UV coverage is 4.2 %. The lower left corner of each image shows the FWHM of the CLEAN beam.

were gain 0.1, threshold 0 Jy, natural weighting; however, the number of CLEAN iterations had to be increased from 500 to 1000 for the first and to 90 000 for the second source in order to obtain satisfying results). For the CLEAN reconstructions, the SNRs are 6.1 dB and 15.9 dB, the dynamic ranges are 17.6 and 121.5, and the RMSE per pixel are 0.12 % and 0.05 % of the true mean intensity for the first and second example, respectively. It is noticeable that for the second example, the Gaussians are not clearly separated from each other.

The compressed sensing reconstructions using a Daubechies wavelet basis, Figure 3.5(c), yield SNRs of 5.0 dB and 6.6 dB, dynamic ranges of 19.2 and 24.6, and RMSE per pixel of 0.13 % and 0.15 % of the true mean intensity. These metrics indicate that the performance of the proposed algorithm is comparable with CLEAN, although not yet on par. The largest contribution to the lower SNR values is due to the occurrence of negative flux regions which are not penalized in the current implementation. In Chapter 5, such unphysical effects are suppressed using a hard constraint, and the gridding process—another source of possibly significant errors—is circumvented.

Visual comparison of the results shows that the compressed sensing algorithm is able to resolve the series of Gaussians, even though some larger scale stripes are present in the background. The computation time of the non-optimized, single-threaded algorithm was about 4.5 s on conventional PC hardware. For comparison, the automatic CLEAN reconstruction took three seconds for the 1000 iterations of the first source, and 160 s for the 90 000 iterations of the second source.

3.6.2 Real data

The applicability of the proposed algorithm to realistic, noise-affected measurements is demonstrated using snapshot observations from the VLA in the 'D' configuration at 14.965 GHz and a UV coverage of 2.4 %. Figure 3.6 shows a series of reconstructions of this dataset containing the Sgr A West region, including the central 'Minispiral'. Figure 3.6(b) shows the reconstruction using CLEAN in CASA with default parameters. This CLEAN result can be considerably improved by manually optimizing the parameters and constraining the intensity to specified regions (commonly referred to as *boxing*). Figure 3.6(c) shows a radio map that was produced by a versed radio astronomer using AIPS in such a user-guided CLEAN session (100 000 iterations, gain 0.1, manual boxing). Finally, Figure 3.6(d) shows the results using ℓ_1-minimization in the pixel basis. All images share a cell size of 1.2″ and are convolved with the CLEAN beam with a FWHM of 10.2″ × 4.3″.

Compressed sensing appears to reconstruct the image better than automated CLEAN, but still shows some systematic imaging effects at lower intensity levels. The dynamic range of the reconstructions is 43.5 for CLEAN with the default parameters, 1367 for user-guided

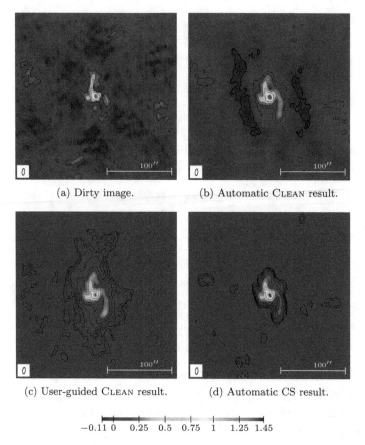

(a) Dirty image.　　　　　　(b) Automatic CLEAN result.

(c) User-guided CLEAN result.　　　(d) Automatic CS result.

Figure 3.6: A radio map of Sgr A West was reconstructed from VLA data using CLEAN with the default parameters (b), CLEAN with user guidance (c), and pixel magnitude minimization (d). Contour levels are plotted at $-1, 1, 2, 4, \ldots, 2^n$ times the respective 3σ RMS noise. The color scale is in arbitrary units, with the peak flux of all images normalized to the same level. All images are cropped to the inner 210×210 pixels (about $250'' \times 250''$), and the UV coverage is 2.4%. The lower left corner of each image shows the FWHM of the CLEAN beam.

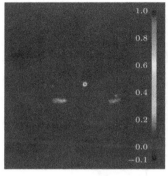 

(a) CLEAN reconstruction.　　　　(b) CS reconstruction.

Figure 3.7: Reconstruction results for the radio source 3C 338 from VLA observations in the 'A' configuration (41 525 visibilities), using CLEAN (a) and compressed sensing (b). CLEAN suffers from striping artifacts and an uneven background. These artifacts are considerably reduced in the compressed sensing reconstruction.

CLEAN and 610 for the proposed approach. The background intensity level required for the computation of the dynamic range was computed from the right quarter of the image. The computation time of the proposed non-optimized, single-threaded algorithm was 9 s on conventional PC hardware, the automatic CLEAN reconstruction took about two seconds, while approximately 15 min were needed for the user-guided reconstruction, including self-calibration steps.

As a second example, the radio source 3C 338 is reconstructed from VLA observations, Figure 3.7(b). When compared to the CLEAN reconstruction result, Figure 3.7(a), compressed sensing features several advantages. The background of the compressed sensing reconstruction appears more even and exhibits less regions of (unphysical) negative pixel intensities. In addition, the low amount of information contained in the data does not result in conspicuous striping artifacts. Instead, the reconstruction error is distributed more evenly across the image. The runtime of both algorithms is about two seconds on a conventional PC, but the compressed sensing algorithm leaves room for optimization and parallelization, in contrast to the inherently sequential CLEAN algorithm.

3.7 Conclusion

The evaluation of the compressed sensing algorithm on simulated and real measurements shows that it is able to provide interferometric image reconstructions that reproduce the main features of complex sources without any manual parameter tweaking or boxing, at comparable computation times as traditional reconstruction algorithms. The method has been proven to converge towards the optimal solution as well as to be stable with respect to noise [Zhu08]. The reconstruction results of this first implementation are still above the observational noise level; however, a number of beneficial constraints and other potential improvements exist that are explored in Chapter 5.

Notably, the method presented in this chapter is not limited to radio interferometry. Many other measurement schemes sample a (potentially sparse) signal in the frequency domain, including optical [AMR+98] and seismic [WDR08] interferometry, optical coherence tomography [VKWP03], holographic microscopy [AHGS06], Fourier transform spectrography [DAB01], magnetic resonance imaging [LDP07], as well as synthetic aperture radar [Sul08] and sonar [HG09]. With appropriate modifications to sampling pattern and sparsity bases, the proposed algorithm could provide a reconstruction approach for these related problems, too.

4 Sparsity Modeling

Astronomical nebulae, Figure 4.1, are among the visually most complex and appealing phenomena known outside the bounds of the Solar System. However, our fixed vantage point on Earth limits us to a single known view of these objects; accurate reconstruction of a volumetric model is impossible from such a limited amount of data. Yet, by making certain assumptions about the three-dimensional structure of the object, it is possible to generate plausible and realistic looking volumetric visualizations from a single image. In particular, the approximate spherical or axial symmetry that many types of astronomical nebulae exibit can be used to infer the missing third dimension using regularized optimization methods.

4.1 Background

Astronomical nebulae are of major interest in astronomy and astrophysics. Since the advent of telescopes, they have been studied and catalogued. Modern research has shed light on their important role in the evolution of the universe: some types of nebulae provide the matter

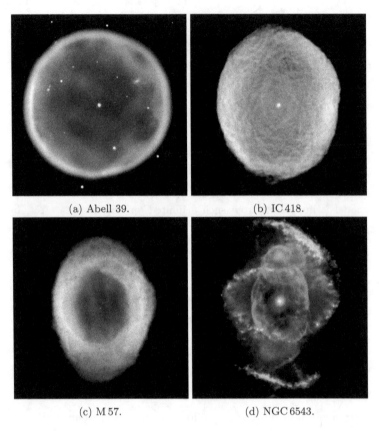

(a) Abell 39.   (b) IC 418.

(c) M 57.   (d) NGC 6543.

Figure 4.1: Different planetary and protoplanetary nebulae.

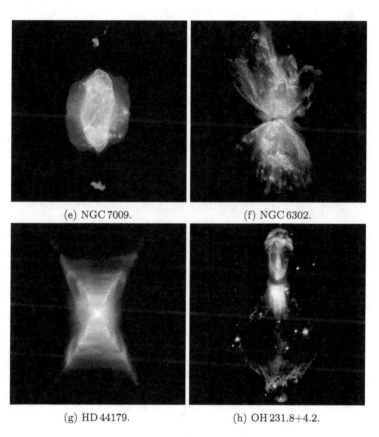

(e) NGC 7009.

(f) NGC 6302.

(g) HD 44179.

(h) OH 231.8+4.2.

Figure 4.1 (continued)

61

from which stars and planetary systems are formed; others, expelled by stars at the end of their lifetime, disperse the heavy elements generated by stellar nucleosynthesis.

Many representatives of the latter class are so-called *planetary nebulae* (or, at an earlier stage, *protoplanetary nebulae*), Figure 4.1, named such because the first observers mistook them for planets due to the limited resolution of their telescopes. More recent observations (e.g., by the Hubble Space Telescope) reveal their often complex and intricate structure [BF02]. Planetary nebulae form when stars of a certain size have used up the hydrogen fuel in their cores and become red giants, inflating to many times their original size. The outer layers of the star are swept away by stellar winds and form an expanding shell. Later, the atoms in the nebula become ionized by ultraviolet radiation from the remaining star, glowing at characteristic wavelengths and observable using optical telescopes. The structure of the resulting nebulae depends on the presence of many factors, including a possible companion star, a strong magnetic field, the surrounding interstellar medium, or internal hydrodynamic effects. Some of these factors favor the formation of rotationally symmetric structures, so that many planetary nebulae exhibit at least an approximate axial symmetry [KS05; Kwo07].

The mechanisms underlying planetary nebula formation and evolution are an active field of research in astrophysics. In addition, their complex and beautiful structure, their important role for the chemical composition of the galaxy, and the fact that our Sun faces a similar fate all have contributed to the fact that planetary nebulae are a popular subject of educational shows in planetariums and dome theaters [MSK+10]. Yet, for such astronomical objects outside our solar system, we can only gather imagery and other observational data from our single point of view. This makes deducing the correct 3D geometry of these objects a notoriously difficult task. Nevertheless, for the purpose of visualization in education and popular science, as in digital full-dome planetariums and sky simulation software such as Celestia [Cel], a plausible and realistic volumetric reconstruction is sufficient. Such a plausible—but not necessarily physically completely accurate—reconstruction can also give astronomers an initial intuition about possible geometries and may serve as a starting point for further manual modeling. For example, it has been shown only recently, using manual modeling, that some classes of nebulae that were believed to be structurally different actually might share a common morphology, but are observed from different vantage points [GDLS+11]. Similar structural intuition could possibly be gained directly from a 3D visualization.

3D information can be obtained from a single image by exploiting the fact that many types of astronomical nebulae exhibit an approximately spherical or axial symmetry. The assumption of approximate symmetry implies that the volumetric model should resemble the known image from all viewpoints that are equivalent to the original viewpoint with

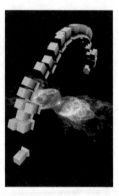

Figure 4.2: Virtual cameras created by rotating the actual camera position about the axis of symmetry all observe similar images (assuming approximate axisymmetry of the object).

respect to the assumed symmetry. For example, in an axisymmetric setting, rotating the camera about the axis of symmetry should not drastically change the image. If the axis of symmetry is not too inclined with respect to the image plane, this allows for a tomographic reconstruction approach in which the original image is replicated at a number of virtual camera positions, Figure 4.2, and a volume is reconstructed by minimizing the reprojection error.

Such tomographic problems are, in principle, amenable to compressed sensing methods. However, several fundamental assumptions of compressed sensing do not hold in this case. The data is likely to be highly inconsistent if the object is not perfectly symmetric, and—depending on the number of virtual projections used—the problem might even be overdetermined. Fortunately, the regularizing term can serve equally well to remove the "noise" generated by inconsistent projections as to resolve ambiguity due to lack of data, so that regularized optimization algorithms can be used to "reconstruct" the volumetric model from a single image using a symmetry assumption.

The approach presented in this chapter features a straightforward workflow. The user selects an image of an astronomical nebula with approximately spherical or axial symmetry from an astronomical image database. Structures that do not belong to the nebula, such as stars, are removed manually. The user then creates a simple setup for the subsequent fully automatic reconstruction by specifying the type of symmetry (along with the symmetry axis or center of symmetry), the desired resolution of the resulting volume, and optional parameters. Afterwards, the reconstruction algorithm solves a constrained optimization problem and computes a volumetric model of the nebula that can be visualized interactively using direct volume rendering [KW03]. The color channels—which either represent the distributions of different ions directly, or are composed for artistic effect—are reconstructed independently.

A fundamental advantage of the proposed method compared to conventional modeling tools is the small number of parameters and their ease of handling: the number of virtual cameras controls the smoothness of the reconstruction; their spatial arrangement is determined by the symmetry of the nebula, with a single additional parameter for jittering. One of the contributions to the core optimization algorithm is to constrain the view from Earth to be similar to the original image; the level of similarity is controlled by a single parameter. A last parameter controls the magnitude of regularization to resolve ambiguities and inconsistencies.

4.2 Related work

Because of the difficulty of deducing plausible three-dimensional structure from a single image, the reconstruction of volumetric models for astronomical nebulae is typically performed manually by astronomers or artists. For example, a complex 3D model of the Orion nebula was created by professional astronomers over several years [NGN+01; ZO95]. Even with specialized modeling tools, the typical modeling time is still measured in weeks and requires skill and astronomical expertise [SKW+11]. Often, a qualitative model is created by an astronomer, and the model parameters are subsequently fitted to the observational data [MFG11; MSGH04; SM06]. Alternatively, by assuming a link between radial velocity and three-dimensional position through a model of nebula evolution, an approximation to the three-dimensional shape can be obtained directly [MFPL04; STR+06]. Due to the difficulty of obtaining spatially resolved spectra, however, the resulting models have low resolution, and the formulation of an appropriate model requires extensive expert knowledge.

Attempts on symmetry-based automatic reconstruction and visualization [Lea91; MKHD04; MKHD05] have produced perfectly symmetric, low-resolution models poor in visual detail. Automated methods for the reconstruction and visualization of asymmetric reflection nebulae [LHM+07; MHLH05] suffer from a similar lack of detail and are not applicable for translucent objects, such as most planetary nebulae. Although it is theoretically possible to introduce artificial asymmetry and detail into the reconstruction results [WAFMM09], this process is as complex as the original reconstruction problem and often results in unappealing visual artifacts like streaks and implausible clusters of emission.

Tomographic reconstruction is common in medical applications such as computed tomography, but can also be used for other transparent volumetric phenomena like flames [IM04]. Iterative reconstruction techniques for computed tomography date back to the 1970s [GBH70]. Since then, numerous iterative reconstruction algorithms have been proposed, including some based on compressed sensing [CBW+10; LDP07; LDSP08; TNC09; YW09]. However, these algorithms are, in general, not suited for large-scale volumetric reconstruction problems with arbitrary projection geometries because the memory requirements for fully volumetric reconstruction algorithms quickly become unmanageable. For example, a 1024^3 32-bit floating-point voxel volume alone requires 4 GB of memory. Accounting for memory occupied by intermediate results, projected images, and previous iterates, the amount of memory raises to about 60 GB for three color channels. Because of these enormous memory requirements of the general volumetric reconstruction problem, many reconstruction algorithms are tailored to specific projection setups to save memory and computation time [JLL+10; SP08; XBMJ03], limiting their range of applicability. The arbitrary projection geometries required for the reconstruction of spherically symmetric nebulae forbid any such optimization. In contrast, the method presented here employs a multi-GPU compute cluster to handle the large quantities of data.

4.3 Image formation and projections

In general, in tomographic applications an object is imaged from several different views from which a discretized volumetric representation of the object can be reconstructed. The imaging process consists in projecting the volume to these views according to an optical model of emission and absorption [Max95]. Many astronomical objects like planetary nebulae exhibit little to no absorption and scattering; By neglecting these effects, image formation can be described by a linear system of equations. The intensity $I = \sum_i x_i l_i$ of an image pixel is a linear combination of the emission densities $x_1, \ldots, x_n$ along the viewing ray, where l_i is the length of the viewing ray segment that falls into the ith volumetric grid cell along the ray. When the emission densities of the volume are written as a vector $\mathbf{x}$ of grid cell intensities and the intensities of the pixels in the kth view are written as a vector $\mathbf{y}_k$ of pixel values, one can define the forward *projection* as a linear operator $\mathbf{M}_k$ such that $\mathbf{M}_k\mathbf{x} = \mathbf{y}_k$. In the following, the term "projection" will be used meaning that the operator computes a projection of a volume into an image or vice versa; it is not related to the mathematical concept of projection operators.

In a typical tomographic application, many images $\mathbf{y}_k$ will be captured. By stacking these image vectors and the corresponding operators $\mathbf{M}_k$, the complete capturing process can be summarized in a system of linear equations

$$\begin{pmatrix} \mathbf{M}_1 \\ \vdots \\ \mathbf{M}_n \end{pmatrix} \mathbf{x} = \begin{pmatrix} \mathbf{y}_1 \\ \vdots \\ \mathbf{y}_n \end{pmatrix}, \quad \text{or} \quad \mathbf{M}\mathbf{x} = \mathbf{y}. \tag{4.1}$$

The transpose of the forward projection operator, the backward projection operator $\mathbf{M}_k^{\mathsf{T}}$, is equally important for the mathematical formulation and the implementation of the algorithm. Intuitively, it distributes the intensity of each pixel among all contributing grid cells proportionally to their contribution. For use in an optimization algorithm, it is imperative that the forward and backward projection operators are exact adjoints of each other. This means that naïve implementations (like interpolation in 3D space by sampling along the ray for the forward projection and interpolation in 2D space by splatting the voxel coordinates for the backward projection) cannot be used. Instead, the integral through a voxel is analytically precomputed (assuming trilinear interpolation). For example, within the positive octant of the unit cube ($x \in [0, 1]$, $y \in [0, 1]$, $z \in [0, 1]$), the contribution of the sample at position $(1, 1, 1)^\mathsf{T}$ to a ray that enters the cube at $(e_x, e_y, e_z)^\mathsf{T}$ and exits at $(e_x + d_x, e_y + d_y, e_z + d_z)^\mathsf{T}$ is

$$
\int_0^1 (e_x + td_x)(e_y + td_y)(e_z + td_z)\, dt
$$
$$
= e_x e_y e_z + \frac{d_x e_y e_z + e_x d_y e_z + e_x e_y d_z}{2}
$$
$$
+ \frac{e_x d_y d_z + d_x e_y d_z + d_x d_y e_z}{3} + \frac{d_x d_y d_z}{4} \ . \quad (4.2)
$$

The contributions of the other voxels adjacent to this unit cube are obtained by inverting the appropriate coordinates in the integral, so that, for example, $e_x + td_x$ becomes $1 - e_x - td_x$ for the voxel at $(0, 1, 1)^\mathsf{T}$. For other locations, the fractional parts of e_x, e_y and e_z are used accordingly.

The forward projection operator $\mathbf{M}_k$ uses a fast voxel traversal algorithm [AW87] to traverse all voxels contributing to a pixel, Figure 4.3(a), whereas the backward projection operator $\mathbf{M}_k^\mathsf{T}$ projects the three-dimensional support of each voxel into the image plane to find the contributing pixels, Figure 4.3(b). Since repeated computation of forward and backward projections is the computational bottleneck of most iterative tomographic reconstruction techniques, both projection

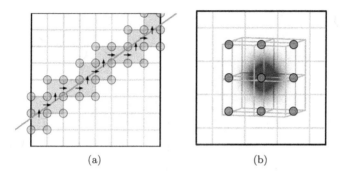

(a)   (b)

Figure 4.3: (a) Traversal for a single output pixel (viewing ray drawn
in red) through the volume data during forward projection
with all contributing voxels marked blue. (b) The weight
distribution of a single voxel (blue) in the backward projection with all contributing pixels (red). In both illustrations,
the affected grid cells of the volume are indicated in green.

operators are distributed among the GPUs in a compute cluster to
speed up this operation and to make use of the combined memory size.

4.4 Symmetry and regularization

In the context of tomographic reconstruction, assumptions about
spatial symmetry can conveniently be modeled by reconstructing the
volume from a number of *virtual views*. For example, a spherically
symmetric object looks the same from every possible viewpoint; this can
be modeled by creating a number of viewpoints *randomly* distributed
on the surface of a sphere (looking at the center), and associating

a copy of the original observed image with each viewpoint. With respect to enforcing exact symmetry using an analytical model, this approach has the advantage of allowing small deviations that create more variety in the visualization and are important for being able to discern different views of the 3D object. A larger number of virtual views create more accurate symmetry, whereas fewer views introduce more variety and a more realistic impression of depth. In addition, the concept of random virtual views flexibly adapts to other types of symmetry. For example, axially symmetric objects can be modeled by arranging the virtual views around the axis of symmetry.

If the virtual views are arranged according to perfect axial symmetry, renderings of the resulting volumes usually do not change much under rotation about the axis of symmetry, and the artificially introduced symmetry might become conspicuous. By randomly perturbing the axis for each individual view by a small amount, additional variance can be introduced so that the perception of depth is preserved when rotating, and the symmetry of the object becomes less striking.

In the present algorithm, the regularizing term is chosen as the ℓ_1-norm of $\mathbf{x}$. This promotes compact objects on a clear low-intensity background, which is a favorable property for the reconstruction of isolated astronomical objects. In addition, this scheme integrates easily with the requirement of nonnegative intensities, in contrast to minimization of the wavelet coefficients, which can lead to overshooting and ringing artifacts (cf. Chapter 3); compared to minimization of the total variation, it is computationally more efficient and preserves fine detail that would easily be suppressed by TV regularization.

4.5 Algorithm

The algorithm presented here is an extension of FISTA, (2.19) and (2.20), adapted to the tomographic reconstruction problem and extended with an option to enforce nonnegativity of intensities as well as additional constraints. It minimizes $\frac{1}{2} \|\mathbf{Mx} - \mathbf{y}\|_2^2 + \|\lambda\mathbf{x}\|_1$ subject to $\mathbf{x} \geq 0$ and $\mathbf{Bx} = \mathbf{c}$, where $\mathbf{BB}^\mathsf{T} = \mathbb{I}$. The complete pseudocode for the algorithm is shown in Algorithm 2.

Constraints of the form $\mathbf{Bx} = \mathbf{c}$ are useful in nebula modeling because one view is known to be exact while all others are potentially subject to inconsistencies. In that case, $\mathbf{B}$ is chosen as a single projection $\mathbf{M}_k$. In the context of a proximal algorithm, hard constraints can be included via the proximal mapping of an indicator function, the orthogonal projection on the set of feasible solutions. Here, the image $\mathbf{c}$ is aligned with the xy-plane of the voxel grid, so that $\mathbf{BB}^\mathsf{T} = \mathbb{I}$ when normalized appropriately. Projections of $\mathbf{x}$ onto $\mathbf{Bx} = \mathbf{c}$ can then be computed explicitly as $\mathbf{x} \leftarrow \mathbf{x} + \mathbf{B}^\mathsf{T}(\mathbf{c} - \mathbf{Bx})$, which can be shown by multiplying with $\mathbf{B}$ from the left. In the present implementation, the hard constraints are enforced by alternately executing a combined gradient-thresholding step and projecting onto $\mathbf{x} \geq 0$ and $\mathbf{Bx} = \mathbf{c}$ in an inner loop comprising n_{inner} iterations (alternatively, a composite

---

Algorithm 2 Modified FISTA algorithm for minimizing $\frac{1}{2}\|\mathbf{M}\mathbf{x} - \mathbf{y}\|_2^2 + \|\lambda\mathbf{x}\|_1$ subject to $\mathbf{x} \geq 0$ and $\mathbf{B}\mathbf{x} = \mathbf{c}$, where $\mathbf{B}\mathbf{B}^\mathsf{T} = \mathbb{I}$.

$L \leftarrow$ largest eigenvalue of $\mathbf{M}^\mathsf{T}\mathbf{M}$

$\mathbf{x}^{(0)} \leftarrow 0,\ \hat{\mathbf{x}}^{(0)} \leftarrow 0,\ t^{(0)} \leftarrow 1$

for $k = 1$ to n_{outer} **do**

$\quad \mathbf{x}^{(k)} \leftarrow \max\left(\hat{\mathbf{x}}^{(k)} - \frac{\mathbf{M}^\mathsf{T}(\mathbf{M}\hat{\mathbf{x}}^{(k-1)} - \mathbf{y})}{L} - \frac{\lambda}{L}, 0\right)$

$\quad$ **for** $j = 1$ to n_{inner} **do**

$\quad\quad \mathbf{x}^{(k)} \leftarrow \mathbf{x}^{(k)} + \mathbf{B}^\mathsf{T}\left(\mathbf{c} - \mathbf{B}\mathbf{x}^{(k)}\right)$

$\quad\quad \mathbf{x}^{(k)} \leftarrow \max\left(\mathbf{x}^{(k)} - \frac{\mathbf{M}^\mathsf{T}(\mathbf{M}\mathbf{x}^{(k)} - \mathbf{y})}{L} - \frac{\lambda}{L}, 0\right)$

$\quad$ **end for**

$\quad t^{(k+1)} \leftarrow \frac{1+\sqrt{1+4t^{(k)2}}}{2}$

$\quad \hat{\mathbf{x}}^{(k+1)} \leftarrow \mathbf{x}^{(k)} + \frac{t^{(k)}-1}{t^{(k+1)}}\left(\mathbf{x}^{(k)} - \mathbf{x}^{(k-1)}\right)$

end for

return $\mathbf{x}^{(n_{\text{outer}})}$

---

proximal mapping [Com09; Yu13b] could be used). The number of iterations specifies the tradeoff between runtime and compliance with the constraints.

For practical reconstruction problems, additional prior information is often given in form of an approximate a priori assumption about the distribution of intensity. For example, if an object is known to be compact, the presence of intensity farther from the center becomes increasingly unlikely. Such prior information can be incorporated in the reconstruction algorithm by replacing the scalar regularization parameter λ by a vector that is multiplied element-wise with $\mathbf{x}$. Thus, a different regularization parameter can be specified for each voxel in $\mathbf{x}$, where smaller values of λ represent a higher a priori probability of intensity in the corresponding voxel. This kind of spatially dependent regularization can lead to much more compact and realistic models with less background noise.

In Algorithm 2, the operators $\mathbf{M}$, $\mathbf{M}^\mathsf{T}$, $\mathbf{B}$, and $\mathbf{B}^\mathsf{T}$ only need to be given implicitly by their matrix-vector products, which can be computed efficiently since $\mathbf{M}$ and $\mathbf{B}$ are projection operators. L is computed from $\mathbf{M}^\mathsf{T}\mathbf{M}$ using the power iteration method (cf. Section 2.2.2). The regularization parameter λ can be a vector to allow for spatially varying regularization. The constraint $\mathbf{B}\mathbf{x} = \mathbf{c}$ is enforced in the inner loop, while nonnegativity is ensured directly in the proximal mapping of the ℓ_1-norm, the positive soft thresholding operator (2.44).

4.6 Results

The accuracy of the algorithm and its applicability to general tomographic reconstruction problems are verified by reconstructing a known test dataset, Figure 4.4(a), from a number of CT-like projections. The reconstruction error declines approximately exponentially with the number of steps, Figure 4.4(c), and after 100 steps the relative squared error $\|\mathbf{x} - \mathbf{x}'\|_2^2 / \|\mathbf{x}\|_2^2$ is about 10^{-3}, where $\mathbf{x}$ is the original volume and $\mathbf{x}'$ is the reconstruction. The reconstructed image shows no visible

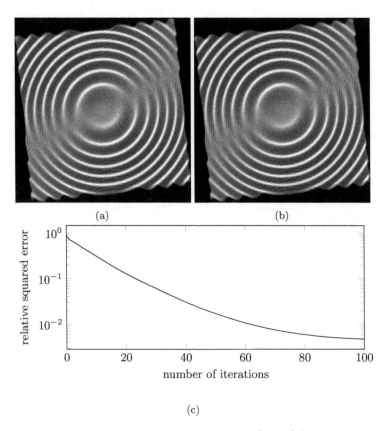

(a)   (b)

(c)

Figure 4.4: The Marschner-Lobb test dataset [ML94] (a) was reconstructed at 128^3 voxels resolution (b) from 128 virtual
cameras distributed evenly around the up axis. The rel-
ative squared error $\|\mathbf{x} - \mathbf{x}'\|_2^2 / \|\mathbf{x}\|_2^2$, computed from the
original volume $\mathbf{x}$ and the reconstruction $\mathbf{x}'$, is plotted logarithmically over the number of steps (c). This experiment
demonstrates the accuracy of the algorithm in a CT-like
setting.

artifacts except for a slight smoothing, Figure 4.4(b). This accuracy is deemed sufficient for the intended application as well as in other fields.

To quantitatively validate the method in its original application domain, it is applied to a single projection, Figure 4.5(a), of a proto-planetary nebula model built manually by an astronomer, Figure 4.5(c). The numerical comparison of the reconstructed volume to the original dataset shows a relative error of about 4.6 %. The value is expected to be higher for nebulae with less pronounced symmetry. An oblique view of the reconstructed model, Figure 4.5(b), shows some weak streaking artifacts that can be suppressed by jittering of the axis, albeit at the cost of a larger numerical error.

To evaluate the visual quality of the results and the performance of the proposed algorithm, reconstructions of several approximately spherically and axially symmetric nebulae were performed. Direct volume rendering is used to visualize the resulting volumetric data. The parallel algorithm was executed on a GPU cluster consisting of 32 physical nodes, each with 2 Intel Xeon X5620 Quad Core CPUs, 2 Nvidia GeForce GTX480 GPUs, and 24 GB RAM. The physical nodes are interconnected over an InfiniBand network with a bandwidth of 20 Gbit s^{-1}. The parallel implementation employs C++ for the host code, CUDA for the GPU code, and mvapich2 for the communication via MPI. An MPI process is deployed for each GPU in the cluster domain to support flexible execution configurations.

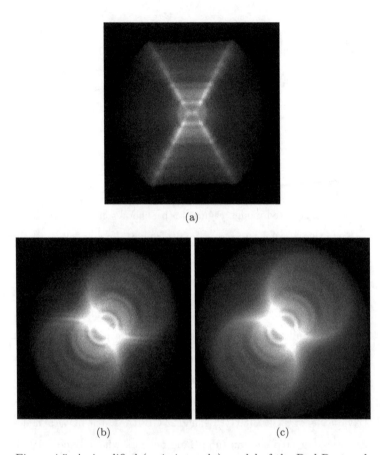

Figure 4.5: A simplified (emission-only) model of the Red Rectangle nebula built manually by an astronomer [KKS11] was rendered to produce a single projection (a). From this image, the model was reconstructed at a resolution of 128^3 voxels using 128 virtual cameras distributed evenly around the up axis. When rendered from a novel viewpoint, the reconstruction (b) is visually quite similar to the original (c); the relative error is about 4.6 %.

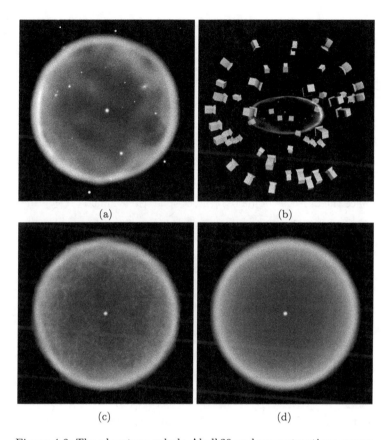

(a) (b)

(c) (d)

Figure 4.6: The planetary nebula Abell 39 and reconstructions assuming spherical symmetry. After removing background stars, the original image (a) was replicated at several virtual camera positions distributed randomly around the center of the object (schematic display in (b)) and subsequently reconstructed at a resolution of 512^3 voxels with $\lambda = 0$ and $n_{\text{outer}} = 40$ for (c) 64 and (d) 512 virtual cameras.

As a first example of actual astronomical imagery, the planetary nebula Abell 39 is considered, Figure 4.6(a). Its geometry resembles a hollow sphere. For its reconstruction, virtual cameras were placed at random locations around the center, Figure 4.6(b). By associating the original image with all of these virtual views, the assumption of spherical symmetry is implicitly defined. The corresponding reconstruction reproduces the supposed geometry of the object with increasing accuracy as the number of projections increases, Figures 4.6(c) and 4.6(d). Since the object is of almost perfect spherical symmetry, the projections are largely consistent and no regularization is needed, so that $\lambda = 0$.

The supernova remnant 0509-67.5 is a nebula with only approximate spherical symmetry, Figure 4.7(a). In the false-color image, visible-light observations from the Hubble Space Telescope (pink and surrounding star field) are combined with X-ray data from the Chandra X-ray Observatory (blue and green). This example illustrates how the proposed algorithm handles arbitrary projection geometries, massively inconsistent projections, equality constraints, and spatial regularization. Again, spherical symmetry is assumed. Since the symmetry is only approximate, the projections are inconsistent, and without further precautions details would be averaged out, Figure 4.7(b). To preserve the familiar appearance of the object from the initial perspective, an equality constraint is used. Location-dependent regularization is introduced to resolve the ambiguity caused by competing projections;

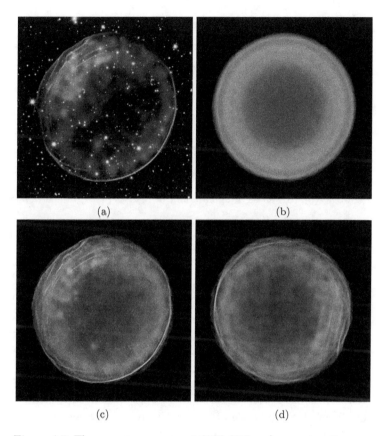

(a)   (b)

(c)   (d)

Figure 4.7: The supernova remnant 0509-67.5 and reconstructions assuming spherical symmetry. After manually removing the
background stars, the original image (a) was replicated at
128 virtual camera positions distributed randomly around
the center of the object as in Figure 4.6(b). Without constraints, the front view bears only a faint resemblance to
the original image (b). With constraints, both front (c)
and novel views (d) exhibit more detail. The volume was
reconstructed at a resolution of 512^3 voxels with $\lambda = 10^3 r$,
$n_{\text{outer}} = 40$, and $n_{\text{inner}} = 2$ in 8592 s.

λ is chosen proportional to the Euclidean distance r of each voxel to the center of symmetry. This regularization not only reduces the amount of voxels with nonzero intensity, thereby suppressing typical artifacts (cf. Figure 4.12); with λ increasing radially from the center, it also favors compact objects, similar to an implicit regularization mechanism used for reconstruction of reflection nebulae [MHLH05]. The result is a consistent and plausible volumetric visualization that is approximately symmetric but retains its resemblance to the original, Figure 4.7(c), as well as a high amount of realistic, fine-grained detail for other vantage points, Figure 4.7(d).

The Butterfly Nebula, or M2–9, is an example of a bipolar planetary nebula whose structure is more accurately described by an approximate axisymmetry, Figure 4.8(a). The axisymmetry can be modeled by distributing the virtual cameras randomly around the axis of symmetry. Only projections from the front are used; projections from the back would be equivalent except for mirroring of the image. Again, the projection from the front is constrained to be similar to the observed image, and the regularization weight λ increases with distance from the symmetry axis. Even though the assumed symmetry is only approximate, most details are clearly visible in the reconstructed volume, Figure 4.8(b). As the point of view approaches the axis, the two-shell structure of the nebula becomes apparent although some detail is inevitably averaged out, Figures 4.8(c) and 4.8(d).

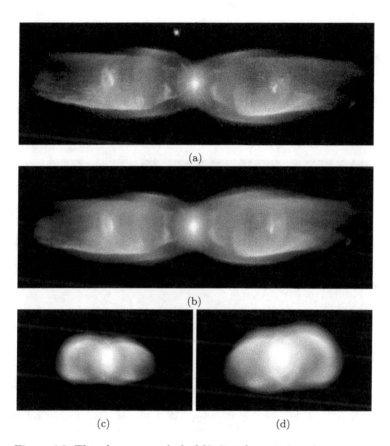

(a)

(b)

(c)   (d)

Figure 4.8: The planetary nebula M2–9 and reconstructions assuming axial symmetry. The reconstruction algorithm uses a single input image (a) to produce a high-resolution 3D visualization that closely resembles the original image when rendered from the same viewpoint (b). From novel vantage points, the emission along the principal axis of the nebula accumulates and creates a luminous halo (c)–(d). The resolution of the reconstructed volume is 512^3 voxels.

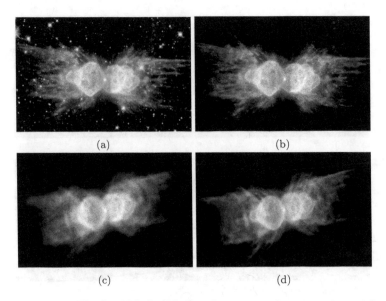

(a)   (b)

(c)   (d)

Figure 4.9: The Ant Nebula (Mz 3) and reconstructions assuming axial
symmetry. After manually removing the background stars,
the original image (a) was replicated at 128 virtual camera positions distributed randomly around the symmetry
axis of the object (see schematic display in Figure 4.2).
To obtain a more natural and less symmetric impression,
the symmetry axis was jittered by $\pm 4°$ for each camera.
Constraining the projection from the front to be similar
to the original image, the volume was reconstructed at a
resolution of 512^3 voxels with $\lambda = 10^3 r$, $n_{outer} = 40$, and
$n_{inner} = 5$ in 9633 s. (b) The resulting view from the front
closely resembles the original image. (c) The oblique view
exhibits less detail but an overall realistic shape. (d) In
contrast, the same view of a model reconstructed from
cameras distributed uniformly around the axis without
jittering looks less realistic, especially when animated, and
suffers from directional artifacts.

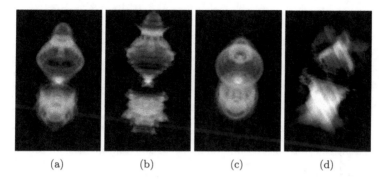

(a)   (b)   (c)   (d)

Figure 4.10: Reconstruction results for the Ant Nebula from previous work: (a)–(c) Constrained Inverse Volume Rendering [MKHD04] and (d) Algebraic 3D Reconstruction
[WAFMM09].

The Ant Nebula, or Mz 3, is another example of a bipolar nebula,
albeit with much more fine structure and less apparent symmetry,
Figure 4.9(a). The cameras are again arranged around the symmetry
axis; to increase the amount of perceived three-dimensionality, the axis
is randomly inclined for each camera so that moving about the axis
produces more visual variation (cf. Figure 4.2). Again, spatially varying
regularization is used, as well as an equality constraint to preserve
the original appearance, Figure 4.9(b). When seen from a novel
viewpoint, Figure 4.9(c), the visualization shows much more detail
and less visible artifacts than previous approaches, Figures 4.10(a)
to 4.10(d). The result appears more realistic—albeit less rich in

detail—than a reconstruction from uniformly distributed cameras, Figure 4.9(d), which is even more obvious in animation.

To demonstrate the importance of equality constraints, consider the Cat's Eye Nebula, or NGC 6543, Figure 4.11(a). It is a rather complex nebula whose shape is believed to consist mainly of an elongated central bubble and two larger spherical lobes [Bal04]. Due to its asymmetry, a simple axisymmetry assumption produces overly symmetric, unrealistic results, Figure 4.11(b). Using an equality constraint for the original projection reproduces the nebula much more accurately, Figure 4.11(c). Novel views, however, reveal that the alleged bispherical geometry is only imperfectly reconstructed; the reconstructed geometry instead resembles a single larger shell, Figures 4.11(d) and 4.11(e).

To study the effects of different amounts of regularization, the planetary nebula NGC 6826, Figure 4.12(a), is reconstructed with different parameters assuming axial symmetry. Without regularization, artifacts arise in the outer regions of the volume, Figure 4.12(b). Moderate regularization entirely removes these artifacts, Figure 4.12(c), and produces a faithful visualization, Figure 4.12(d), that looks plausible also from novel viewpoints, Figure 4.12(e). Although the range of suitable values of λ comprises several orders of magnitude, excessively large values can lead to darkening of the outer parts of the object, Figure 4.12(f). In practice, the same value of λ is appropriate for a wide range of objects, and the effects of too small or too large a value are easily recognized by comparison with the original image.

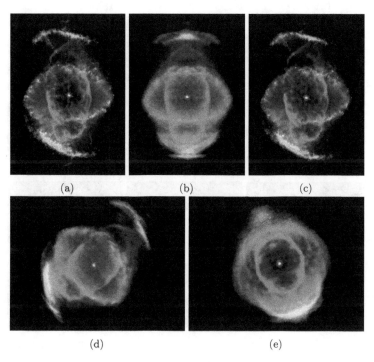

(a)   (b)   (c)

(d)   (e)

Figure 4.11: The Cat's Eye Nebula (NGC 6543) and reconstructions
assuming axial symmetry. The original image (a) was
replicated at 128 virtual camera positions distributed
randomly around the symmetry axis of the object as in
Figure 4.2, again with jittering about $\pm 4°$ at a resolution
of 512^3 voxels with $\lambda = 10^3 r$. (b) Without constraining
the projection from the front, the result is overly symmetric. (c) Enabling constraints with $n_{inner} = 5$ results in a
more convincing reconstruction by introducing asymmetric features. (d) Rotating the constrained model toward
the axis of symmetry still shows asymmetric features. (e)
As the vantage point approaches the symmetry axis, the
apparent shape of the Cat's Eye nebula changes more
toward a ring nebula.

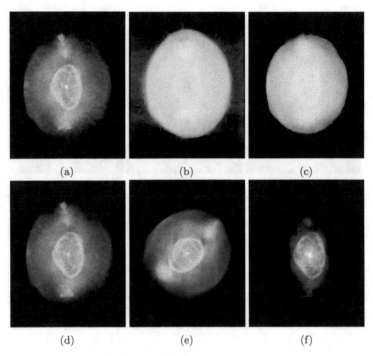

Figure 4.12: Analysis of regularization parameter λ with reconstructions of planetary nebula NGC 6826. The original image (a) was replicated at 128 virtual camera positions distributed randomly around the symmetry axis of the object, again with jittering about $\pm 4°$. (b) Without regularization, by setting $\lambda = 0$, noise and streaking are evident, here displayed with logarithmically scaled intensity to make them clearly visible. (c) Employing our regularization approach with $\lambda = 10^3 r$. reduces noise and streak artifacts significantly at the same intensity scaling. (d) With linearly scaled intensity, the reconstruction closely reproduces the original image and also remains plausible when seen from a different vantage point (e). (f) In contrast, if the regularization factor is chosen much too large (here $\lambda = 5 \times 10^4 r$), the outer parts of the nebula become suppressed.

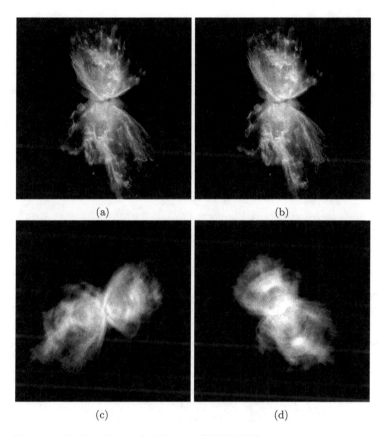

(a)   (b)

(c)   (d)

Figure 4.13: The Butterfly Nebula (NGC 6302) and reconstructions
assuming axial symmetry. The original image (a) was
replicated at 128 virtual camera positions distributed
randomly around the symmetry axis of the object as in
Figure 4.2, again with jittering about $\pm 4°$ at a resolution
of 512^3 voxels with $\lambda = 10^3 r$. This is a typical failure
case of the algorithm as the large amounts of dust in the
nebula violate the assumption of pure emission. While
the rendering from the original vantage point is able to
reproduce the input image accurately (b), oblique views
do not reproduce the expected absorption at the tips of
the two main lobes (c)–(d).

4.7 Limitations

Figure 4.13 shows a failure case of the algorithm. The outer regions of the Butterfly nebula apparently contain both absorption and scattering, neither of which are compatible with the basic assumptions presented in Section 4.3. These regions are therefore not interpreted as emissive regions attenuated by an absorbing layer, but as empty space. While the original view can be reproduced, Figure 4.13(b), oblique views exhibit missing parts, and their appearence differs significantly from the expected structure, Figures 4.13(c) and 4.13(d).

4.8 Conclusion

The results show that the proposed tomographic algorithm is capable of reconstructing volumes of resolutions up to 512^3 voxels from up to 512 projections in a fully automatic way. When presented with strongly inconsistent, contrived projections in the context of astronomical nebula reconstruction from single images, a regularization scheme preserves the plausibility of the result.

Astronomical nebulae of roughly spherical shape were shown to be faithfully modeled by the algorithm, retaining a high amount of detail and present irregularities in the geometry. Axisymmetric objects, on the other hand, lose some detail when the camera approaches the symmetry axis. Here, the generation of synthetic detail may provide a remedy in the future. However, the additional constraints not only help reproduce the original view convincingly, but also reconstruct crucial asymmetric features that convey a realistic impression of irregularity even when the viewpoint is close to the axis. In fact, the models shown in this chapter have quickly been adopted by the planetarium community and are included in recent releases of commercial planetarium software like Evans & Sutherland *Digistar*^{TM} [Dig], SCISS *Uniview*^{TM} [Uni], and RSA Cosmos *SkyExplorer*^{TM} [Sky].

Since the model only reconstructs emission, nebulae that contain a significant amount of scattering or absorption are reconstructed poorly. Reconstructions including simultaneous emission and absorption require nonlinear optimization and are in general more computationally intensive. The *attenuated ray transform* [NW01] may provide a starting point for a model comprising emission and absorption but no scattering: one notes that the change in the intensity $I(x)$ along the viewing ray in the presence of absorption $a(x)$ and emission $e(x)$ is described by $\mathrm{d}I(x)/\mathrm{d}x = -a(x)I(x) + e(x)$, which is solved by $I(x) = I(0)\exp\left(-\int_0^x a(t)\,\mathrm{d}t\right) + \int_0^x e(t)\exp\left(-\int_t^x a(s)\,\mathrm{d}s\right)\mathrm{d}t$. The inverse problem could, in principle, be solved using ℓ_1 minimization algorithms [BBL+07]. Recent grid-free methods [GKHH12] may also provide a method to solve this problem efficiently. In contrast, if scattering is taken into account, every voxel potentially influences the intensity of every image pixel, and the inherent sparsity of the projection operator $\mathbf{M}$ is lost. High-resolution reconstruction of scattering nebulae may be possible using multi-resolution methods that are already used for rendering [MHLH05]. In cases where the scattering effects can be approximated by a convolution in the image plane, the problem could probably be solved by a modified version of the algorithm, but convergence is likely to be considerably slower. In any case, the additional degrees of freedom introduced with absorption and scattering would probably require supplementary regularization terms to resolve the added ambiguity.

The quality of the reconstruction is naturally limited by the fact that the algorithm has no knowledge about the physical processes underlying the objects being reconstructed. Since the algorithm provides a mechanism for specifying additional constraints in a generic way, it would, in theory, be possible to restrict the search space to solutions compatible with a physical model. Additionally, an interactive volumetric reconstruction tool could let the user guide the automatic reconstruction by specifying the position of substructures in space [BKW08] or by manipulating individual views [RWF+13]. Obviously, an interactive editor would require further acceleration of the reconstruction algorithm and live display of intermediate results.

5 Group Sparsity Reconstruction

Radio interferometers can achieve high spatial resolution for temporally constant sources by combining data observed over extended periods of time (cf. Chapter 3). For temporally varying sources, the data from different times cannot be combined directly, but the temporal variation must be taken into account in the data model. For example, recent imaging algorithms reconstruct smoothly varying sources by representing temporal variation in polynomial or Fourier bases [Rau12; SFM11]. In this chapter, a novel image reconstruction algorithm is presented that is able to reconstruct erratically varying sources as well as continuous ones, as long as the variations are confined to small regions of the image. This is achieved by enforcing sparsity of temporal variation through a group sparsity prior. Numerical experiments show that the proposed approach recovers image series to high accuracy where methods without temporal consistency fail, and that it outperforms static reconstructions of dynamic scenes even in image regions with no temporal variation.

5.1 Background

Radio interferometers sample an image of the sky in the Fourier domain with a slowly changing pattern due to the rotation of the Earth. When the sky region being imaged is constant over the time of observation, the different sampling patterns can be combined to produce a single high-quality, high-resolution image. Dynamic sources, however, cannot be imaged in this way with traditional reconstruction methods. On the one hand, if each time frame $\mathbf{x}(t)$ is reconstructed separately from only a small amount of data, the quality of each time frame suffers. On the other hand, if a single image $\mathbf{x}$ is reconstructed from all available data, not only is all temporal resolution lost, but the transient sources can even cause artifacts also in static parts of the image.

In Chapter 3, compressed sensing was used to reconstruct static radio images by finding the sparsest (in some basis) image explaining the data, for example, the one with the fewest nonzero pixels. In this chapter, this idea is extended to simultaneously minimize the number of nonzero pixels and the number of pixels that change over time, without restricting the type of temporal variation that these pixels exhibit. In this way, static image regions benefit from the large amount of information collected during a long observation time, while dynamic image regions are reconstructed at high temporal resolution. Since all pixels are coupled in the data through the Fourier transform, a better reconstruction of the dynamic parts reduces the likelihood of artifacts in static regions, and vice versa.

5.2 Related work

A discussion of reconstruction algorithms for interferometric data in the static setting is found in Section 3.2. For dynamic settings, relatively few methods are known that reconstruct all time slices simultaneously from all available data. Recent algorithms model the temporal variation of each image pixel as Taylor polynomials [Rau12] or Fourier series [SFM11], exploiting the fact that many sources change continuously over time. This allows for the reconstruction of scenes where large regions of the image vary slowly. In many cases, however, most image regions do not change at all, while some localized features may vary erratically. In these cases, methods that describe every pixel by a continuous variation over time suffer from two problems: the erratic temporal variation of the transient region is not represented well in a continuous basis, and at the same time static regions are allowed to vary over time when they really should not change.

5.3 Group sparsity regularization

A significant part of the contribution of this chapter consists in finding a regularizer f that appropriately describes the expected types of transient signals. In order to be applicable to interferometry problems, f should also be approximately orthogonal to the Fourier basis in which visibilities are measured, so that the regularization term actually resolves ambiguities instead of competing with the data term. Finally, to guarantee acceptable runtimes, the proximal mapping for f must be efficient to compute.

The following reasoning is based on the assumption that in a typical radio image containing transients, most pixels exhibit little or no temporal variation. Pixels that do show temporal fluctuations, however, may do so in an erratic manner that appears discontinuous when observed at the typical temporal resolution of a radio interferometer. Therefore, one major objective in the choice of f is to minimize the number of transient pixels, while the exact temporal behavior of these pixels is of lesser importance.

Besides controlling the temporal dependencies between time frames, the regularizer has to enforce the plausibility of each image $\mathbf{x}(t)$ in the time series. In Chapter 3, this was achieved by making use of the fact that many radio images consist of small, isolated objects on a dark background. The pixels of such images are sparsely populated, so that the identity is a reasonable choice for a sparsity basis: minimizing the ℓ_1-norm of the image $\mathbf{x}$ effectively minimizes the number of nonzero pixels, allowing sharp features with high local contrast. When mostly smooth regions of extended emission are present, however, a wavelet basis typically provides a sparser representation. While either approach may be more appropriate depending on the signal being imaged, minimization of wavelet coefficients is prone to undershooting around bright features, resulting in regions of obviously unphysical negative intensity. ℓ_1-norm minimization, on the other hand, can easily be combined with a constraint to enforce nonnegative pixel values. In addition, the ℓ_1-norm is maximally incoherent with the Fourier basis in which the measurements are taken (cf. Section 2.1.4).

The idea of ℓ_1-norm minimization can be generalized to *group sparsity* methods [FR08]. Assume all values of a pixel x_i at different times t are summarized in a group. One wants to minimize the number of groups containing nonzero intensities, but does not care how many of the components in the group are nonzero. This kind of group sparsity can be achieved by minimizing the ℓ_1-norm of the ℓ_∞-norms of all groups, the $\ell_{1,\infty}$-norm $\|\mathbf{x}(t)\|_{1,\infty} = \sum_i \max_t |x_i(t)|$.

When only a single time slice is present, the $\ell_{1,\infty}$-norm obviously degrades to an ℓ_1-norm of $\mathbf{x}$, and the proposed approach becomes equivalent to previous approaches based on ℓ_1-norm minimization. For time-resolved data, however, a number of interesting effects can be observed. First of all, minimizing the number of nonzero groups promotes pixel sparsity of each time slice. In addition, since only the maximum intensity over time is taken into account, erratic temporal behavior of intensity *amplitudes* can be reconstructed. At the same time, temporal consistency of intensity *locations* is achieved: if a pixel is bright in one time frame, the optimal choice for placing ambiguous intensity in another frame is the same pixel, and vice versa. This works because the observational data is only ambiguous with respect to space, not with respect to time (the measurement operator is block-diagonal, and information from different time frames is never mixed). In this way, information from multiple observations with different baseline patterns is effectively combined to resolve ambiguities and to reduce sidelobes in *all* time frames. Similarly, a short flare of an otherwise faint but temporally varying source helps localize the faint source over the total duration of the observation, at the same time preventing the faint source from erroneously showing up as a side lobe in other frames. Finally, if $\ell_{1,\infty}$ minimization is applied to a time-resolved observation of a scene without any temporal variation, one can expect results very similar to those of a direct ℓ_1 reconstruction of a single image from all available data.

5.4 Algorithm

The implementation follows the algorithm outlined in (2.19) and (2.20), with the vectors $\mathbf{x}$, $\hat{\mathbf{x}}$, and $\mathbf{y}$ redefined as their concatenated values from each time frame. Likewise, the measurement operator $\mathbf{M}$ becomes a block-diagonal matrix consisting of the respective Fourier transforms in each time frame. The regularizer $f(\mathbf{x}) = \lambda \left\|\mathbf{x}\right\|_{1,\infty}$ contains implicit information about which components of $\mathbf{x}$ belong to which time frame.

The FISTA algorithm expects real-valued data. Complex numbers, which occur in the visibility data, are therefore represented as tuples consisting of their real and imaginary parts, so that $\mathbf{y} \in \mathbb{C}^n$ is internally represented as $\mathbf{y} \in \mathbb{R}^{2n}$.

In order to be able to use fast Fourier transforms to compute matrix-vector products involving $\mathbf{M}$, the visibility samples need to be splatted onto a regular grid. The error introduced by this gridding is minimized by a *nonequispaced fast Fourier transform* [KKP09], which approximates the actual grid-free Fourier transform with arbitrary accuracy using appropriate window functions and an oversampled fast Fourier transform.

The proximal mapping $p_{\beta\lambda\|\cdot\|_{1,\infty}}(\mathbf{x})$ can be computed independently for each group, i.e., the $\ell_{1,\infty}$-norm is *group separable* (cf. Section 2.3.4). This is because the groups, each consisting of all time frames for a single pixel, are disjoint, and the proximal mapping for the outer ℓ_1-norm is separable in its components as discussed above. The proximal mapping for the inner ℓ_∞-norm,

$$p_{\beta\lambda\|\cdot\|_\infty}(\mathbf{x}) = \arg\min_{\mathbf{w}} \frac{1}{2} \|\mathbf{w} - \mathbf{x}\|_2^2 + \beta\lambda \max_i |w_i| \ , \qquad (5.1)$$

can be computed by projecting $\mathbf{x}$ orthogonally onto the set of all $\mathbf{x}$ with $\|\mathbf{x}\|_1 \leq \beta\lambda$ and subtracting the result from $\mathbf{x}$ (cf. Section 2.3.3). For computing the orthogonal projection, an $\mathcal{O}(n \log n)$ algorithm [DFL08, Lemma 4.2] is used (for a detailed discussion, see [FR08, Lemma 4.2c]).

In order to ensure nonnegativity of the result, any negative values are removed by thresholding $\mathbf{x}$ against zero before applying the proximal mapping as proposed in Section 2.3.3.

For comparison to the proposed method, several variants of the algorithm presented in Chapter 3 are implemented. The *static* method produces a single time frame from all available data under the assumption that the source is temporally constant. The ℓ_1 method reconstructs subsequent time frames individually from the data taken during the respective time frame. Finally, a novel variant, the ℓ_2 method, is implemented. It promotes *smooth temporal variation* in addition to ℓ_1 sparsity of each time frame by extending the ℓ_1 method with a penalty term that is quadratic in the temporal derivative $\partial_t \mathbf{x}$, yielding the problem

$$\arg\min_{\mathbf{x}} \frac{1}{2} \left\| \mathbf{Mx} - \mathbf{y} \right\|_2^2 + \frac{\mu}{2} \left\| \partial_t \mathbf{x} \right\|_2^2 + \lambda \left\| \mathbf{x} \right\|_1 \quad \text{s.t.} \quad \mathbf{x} \geq 0 . \qquad (5.2)$$

The parameter μ controls the strength of temporal smoothing. The above statements on transitioning from the static to the time-dependent case apply. The temporal derivative is approximated by $(\partial_t \mathbf{x})_i (t) = x_i(t) - x_i(t-1)$, where $t > 0$ is an integer index. The problem can be reformulated as

$$\arg\min_{\mathbf{x}} \frac{1}{2} \left\| \begin{pmatrix} \mathbf{M} \\ \mu \partial_t \end{pmatrix} \mathbf{x} - \begin{pmatrix} \mathbf{y} \\ 0 \end{pmatrix} \right\|_2^2 + \lambda \left\| \mathbf{x} \right\|_1 , \qquad (5.3)$$

which can be solved with only minor modifications to the ℓ_1 minimization algorithm.

5.5 Results

The reconstruction accuracy of the proposed method is evaluated on a number of simulated measurements, so that comparison to ground truth data as well as to other reconstruction methods is possible. In addition, a numerical experiment is used to investigate the circumstances under which the proposed method yields significant advantages over existing approaches.

16 subsequent 30-minute observations of different synthetic 32×32 pixel images on a hypothetical 12-antenna array were simulated, yielding 66 visibilities per time frame, Figure 5.1 (left column). The sampling pattern changes over time because of the rotation of the Earth. Images were reconstructed from this data using four different approaches. The *static* reconstruction is similar to a CLEAN reconstruction of a single image from all time frames, while the ℓ_1 reconstruction corresponds to the same method applied to each individual time frame. The ℓ_2 method recreates the effect of an algorithm that assumes smooth temporal variation. Finally, the proposed $\ell_{1,\infty}$ approach promotes sparsity of both the spatial intensity distribution and the set of transient pixels. Reconstructions were also performed using MS-CLEAN [Cor08] and MS-TV-CLEAN [Rau12], which correspond closely to the

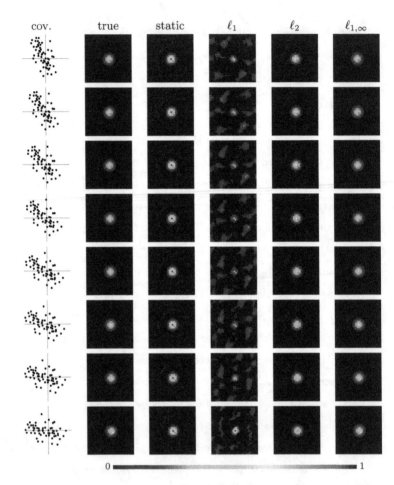

Figure 5.1: Extended source with a smoothly varying transient (second column), reconstructed using different methods (third to last column). The coverage of the array is shown in the first column. Time increases from top to bottom.

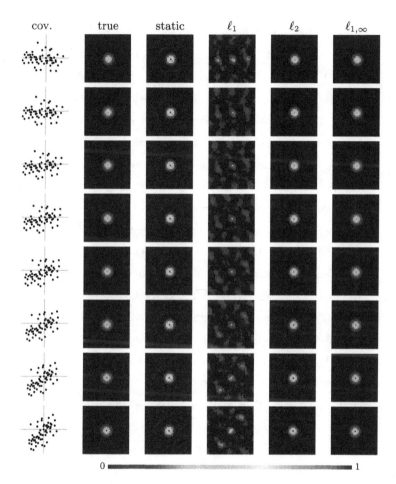

Figure 5.1 (continued)

static and ℓ_2 approaches, respectively; the results are therefore not displayed here. All algorithms were run for 10 000 iterations with $\lambda = 0.1$ and (for ℓ_2) $\mu = 1$. Results did not change significantly for different values of λ and μ within a few orders of magnitude.

For the first experiment, a small moving object on an extended background is simulated. The background is modeled by a cosine-shaped blob, overlaid by a single bright pixel moving diagonally into the center, Figure 5.1 (second column). The static reconstruction (third column) recovers the main features of the source, but is unable to temporally resolve the movement. The ℓ_1 reconstruction (fourth column), on the other hand, suffers from severe artifacts because each individual time frame does not contain enough information to reconstruct the whole image. The ℓ_2 method (fifth column) is well adapted to the continuous type of temporal variation and therefore reconstructs the scene well. However, it does not strongly penalize smooth temporal variation even in static parts of the image, leading to faint sidelobes in the background. Finally, the $\ell_{1,\infty}$ reconstruction (last column) is visually almost indistinguishable from ground truth.

Relative reconstruction errors for the different approaches are shown in Figure 5.2. Because the static method only reconstructs a single time slice, it converges quickly. However, a significant error remains due to the temporally varying parts of the image. The independent reconstructions of the ℓ_1 method converge at similar speed, but leave an even higher error due to the data-starved setting. For the ℓ_2 approach,

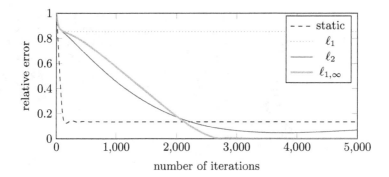

Figure 5.2: Relative errors for the different reconstructions shown in Figure 5.1.

the sidelobes in the background and slight temporal fluctuations in static regions, even when not visually conspicuous, lead to noticeable residual error. Finally, the $\ell_{1,\infty}$ method converges more slowly at first, but finally reaches a relative error of the order of 10^{-4}.

A second experiment investigates how the different approaches perform in the presence of static, smoothly varying and erratically varying sources. The synthetic source consists of a dark background with randomly placed point sources, 30 of which are static, 15 change linearly over time and 15 vary erratically, Figure 5.3 (second column). While the static method (third column) recovers the locations and average intensities of both static and varying sources reasonably well in most cases, visibility data that is not explained by the static model leads to faint bogus sources in background regions. The ℓ_1 method

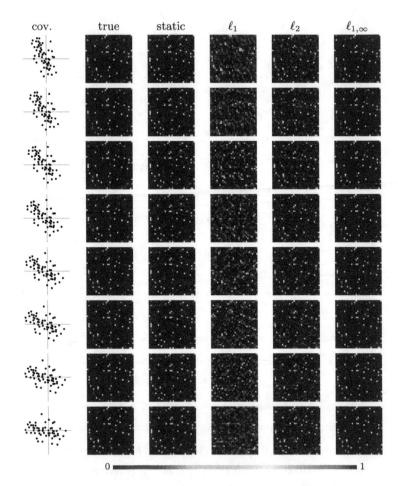

Figure 5.3: Static, smoothly varying and erratic point sources (second column), reconstructed using different methods (third to last column). The coverage of the array is shown in the first column. Time increases from top to bottom.

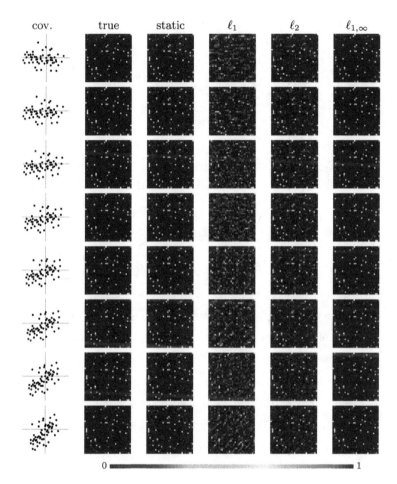

Figure 5.3 (continued)

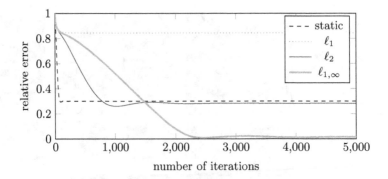

Figure 5.4: Relative errors for the different reconstructions shown in Figure 5.3.

(fourth column) correctly localizes many of the sources; but without exploiting temporal coherence, each individual frame does not contain enough information to be completely reconstructed. The ℓ_2 method (fifth column) reconstructs many static or smoothly varying sources rather well, but attenuates the temporal variation of erratically varying sources. Similar to the static method, this leads to bogus sources in the background. In addition, even many static sources fluctuate slightly over time because no penalty is used to enforce their being completely static. Finally, the $\ell_{1,\infty}$ method (last column) correctly recovers the location and behavior of static, smoothly varying and erratic sources with only minor errors in the absolute intensities.

Relative reconstruction errors for the different approaches are shown in Figure 5.4. The static and ℓ_1 performance resembles the previous experiment, albeit the residual error for the static method is higher due to a larger amount of temporally varying sources. Like the static method, the ℓ_2 approach suffers from artifacts due to visibility data from erratic sources that cannot be explained by the model. It reaches a slightly lower reconstruction error, presumably because the smoothly varying sources are better reproduced. Finally, the $\ell_{1,\infty}$ method correctly localizes all sources, but the bias introduced by the regularization term leads to inaccuracies in absolute intensity of about one percent. This over-regularization can be counterbalanced with a subsequent *debiasing* step that keeps all zero pixels fixed and solves for the remaining intensities in a least-squares sense (cf. Section 2.2.5).

The performance of different reconstruction approaches can vary widely for different observation situations. While a comprehensive quantitative study of the influence of image content on reconstruction quality is beyond the scope of this work, one can investigate how quality varies with the amount of available information per time frame. To do so, the same setup as before is used, but only a random subset of all available visibilities in each frame are selected. Then, several different, randomly generated source images are reconstructed from this shortened data using the four abovementioned methods. By varying the number of visibilities retained in the data, one can graph the relationship between the amount of available information and the reconstruction quality of different algorithms.

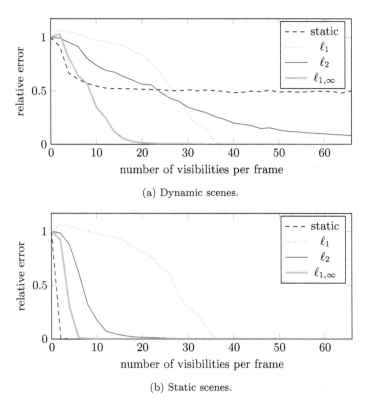

(a) Dynamic scenes.

(b) Static scenes.

Figure 5.5: Median relative errors when reconstructing randomly generated scenes from different numbers of measurements. For dynamic signals (a), the proposed $\ell_{1,\infty}$ approach needs far less information to accurately reconstruct the image than previous approaches. For static signals (b), it is outperformed only by the *static* algorithm, which exploits the prior knowledge that the signal is, in fact, static.

Figure 5.5(a) shows the median relative error computed from reconstructions of 20 source images, each containing 10 randomly placed, erratically varying point sources on a dark background. The ℓ_1 method is able to reconstruct each frame individually (without exploiting temporal coherence) from about 35 visibilities per frame, while the proposed $\ell_{1,\infty}$ approach achieves the same accuracy with as few as 20 visibilities. The ℓ_2 method fails to reach high accuracy because it inevitably smoothes out the erratic variation. Reconstructing a single image using the *static* method fails completely since the scene is dynamic and cannot be represented by a single image. In conclusion, the $\ell_{1,\infty}$ method always performs comparably to the best competitor, independent of the number of visibilities used. However, since it involves a comparatively high computational load, the static or ℓ_1 approaches may be more convenient to use for very low and very high numbers of visibilities, respectively.

After demonstrating that the proposed $\ell_{1,\infty}$ approach is always at least on par with the reference methods for erratic sources, it is investigated how it performs when no temporal variation is present in the data. The results are shown in Figure 5.5(b), where 20 randomly generated images were reconstructed, each containing 10 randomly placed static point sources. First, one observes that the ℓ_1 performance on a static scene is indistinguishable from that on a dynamic scene because the temporal coherence between frames is not exploited. The $\ell_{1,\infty}$ approach, on the other hand, benefits from the additional coherence; satisfactory reconstruction quality is reached with as few as 10 visibilities. The ℓ_2 method requires about 20 visibilities to achieve similar accuracy. This might be caused by the fact that pixel intensities are allowed to fluctuate over time because neither sparsity of the set of transient pixels nor of the temporal variation itself are enforced. Not surprisingly, the *static* method excels at reconstructing a static scene. Unless the number of visibilities is very low, however, the performance of the proposed $\ell_{1,\infty}$ approach is comparable to the *static* reconstruction method even on completely static images; for more than 20 visibilities, the performance of both algorithms is virtually indistinguishable.

To evaluate the robustness of the various approaches in the presence of noise, the experiments were repeated with normally distributed random noise added to the data, Figure 5.6. The standard deviation of the noise is chosen such that the signal-to-noise ratio $\sigma_{\mathrm{signal}}^2/\sigma_{\mathrm{noise}}^2$ is 100, or 20 dB. To account for the nonzero noise level, the influence of the regularization term was raised by increasing the regularization parameter to $\lambda = 1$. In the dynamic case, Figure 5.6(a), the relative performance of the different methods is similar to the noise-free case. All methods suffer from increased reconstruction error, but again, the $\ell_{1,\infty}$ method outperforms all other approaches; this effect is most pronounced for low numbers of visibilities. As more data is added, both the absolute errors and the differences between the methods gradually decrease. In the static case, Figure 5.6(b), as in the noise-free case,

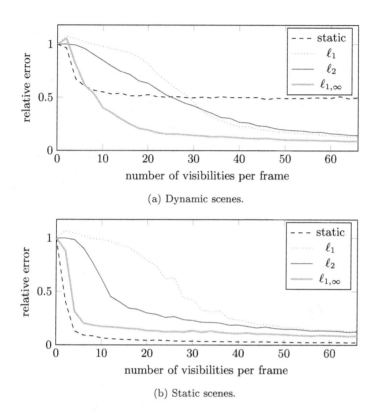

(a) Dynamic scenes.

(b) Static scenes.

Figure 5.6: Median relative errors when reconstructing randomly generated scenes from different numbers of measurements with
a signal-to-noise ratio of 20 dB. The regularization parameter was increased to $\lambda = 1$ to boost the denoising effect.
For low number of visibilities, the error levels are almost
unchanged with respect to the noise-free case. For high
number of visibilities, all methods are similarly affected by
the noise and converge to a common error level, with the
notable exception of the *static* method, which in the static
case profits from redundancy in the data by exploiting the
prior knowledge that the signal is static.

the *static* algorithm outperforms all other methods by making use of the prior knowledge that the signal is static: its error is only about 28% of that of the $\ell_{1,\infty}$ method. The ℓ_2 and $\ell_{1,\infty}$ methods both suffer from erroneous temporal variation but slowly converge to the correct solution as more data is added. As in the noise-free case, the $\ell_{1,\infty}$ approach outperforms both other dynamic reconstruction schemes.

5.6 Conclusion

This chapter has presented a novel image reconstruction algorithm for transient radio sources based on group sparsity. Numerical experiments show that the proposed approach outperforms existing methods on data-starved observations of sources with a sparse pattern of smooth or erratic temporal variation. Outside this realm, it degrades gracefully: for data-starved observations of static scenes, its performance is comparable to sparse reconstruction of a single static image, while for data-rich observations of dynamic scenes, it performs comparably to sparse reconstruction of individual frames. The performance degradation in the presence of noise is similar for all tested methods.

A major limitation of the present approach is the considerable runtime compared to simpler methods, which disallowed an evaluation on large problems comprising real interferometric data (as in Chapter 3). This is partly due to the expensive evaluation of the nonequispaced fast Fourier transforms, which grid and de-grid the visibility data in each iteration. When efficiency is more important than accuracy, the algorithm can instead be applied to pre-gridded data, so that conventional fast Fourier transforms can be used. The main bottleneck of the present implementation, however, is the algorithm for projections onto the ℓ_1-ball: the computation for the test scenes in Figures 5.1 and 5.3 took 20 s, 72 s, and 83 s for the static, ℓ_1, and ℓ_2 methods, respectively. The $\ell_{1,\infty}$ reconstructions, on the other hand, took 881 s for Figure 5.1 and 686 s for Figure 5.3. Chapter 6 presents an approach to compute these projections in $\mathcal{O}(n)$ expected time, bringing the $\ell_{1,\infty}$ computation times for Figures 5.1 and 5.3 down to 446 s and 470 s, respectively.

An obvious extension of the algorithm would be to allow for the reconstruction of multi-frequency data: modern interferometers allow recording data from many frequency bands at once. Since the Fourier domain sampling pattern scales with the observed wavelength, each frequency band contains novel information, so that higher reconstruction quality can be achieved by combining data from different frequency bands. When the image changes with wavelength, multi-frequency reconstruction is desirable to provide additional physical insight, and beneficial effects on reconstruction quality could be obtained from a simultaneous multi-frequency reconstruction by exploiting correlations between the frequency channels using an appropriate group sparsity prior. Multi-frequency imaging is independent of time-resolved imaging, so that both approaches could be straightforwardly combined.

The major challenge in this case would be the handling of the immense amounts of data created by a long-term measurement with high resolution in both time and frequency.

Finally, in order to achieve practical utility in the astronomical community, integration of the reconstruction algorithm with software packages such as CASA is desirable, and would simplify further evaluation of the method on real observational data.

6 Group Sparsity Modeling

In Chapter 4, an approach was presented to reconstruct a volumetric 3D model of an astronomical nebula using the approximate symmetry inherent to many such nebulae. However, this approach requires several hours of computation time even on large multi-GPU clusters. This chapter presents a novel reconstruction algorithm based on group sparsity that reaches or even exceeds the quality of the prior results while taking only a fraction of the time on a conventional desktop PC. In this way, planetarium show designers, presenters, and educators can create their own high-quality volumetric content on commodity hardware that is already present or affordable for end users. As in Chapter 4, the method usually requires no user input aside from a single image obtained from a public database on the internet and an approximate axis of symmetry.

6.1 Background

In this chapter, it will be shown that group sparsity methods like the one presented in Chapter 5 can be used to promote symmetry without the need for virtual projections. The symmetry properties of a voxelized volume are described by defining a set G of disjoint groups $g \in G$ of voxels so that in a symmetric volume, the voxels within each group have equal intensities. A group sparsity regularizer based on these groups is then used to promote symmetry in the reconstruction.

In the case of axial symmetry, the groups are concentric rings, Figure 6.1: the voxels are binned according to the distance of their center from the axis of symmetry and its position along the axis. However, any configuration of disjoint sets can be used. In principle, this makes it possible to model arbitrary symmetries such as spherical symmetries, discrete rotational symmetries, mirror symmetries, translational symmetries, or rotational symmetries about arbitrarily shaped (e.g., curved) axes.

6.2 Related work

A discussion of automatic modeling algorithms for astronomical nebulae is found in Section 4.2. While the automatic modeling method presented in Chapter 4 has resulted in seven high-resolution models that have quickly been embraced by several vendors of planetarium software for use in their commercial digital full-dome visualization systems, their creation requires long computation times on a large multi-GPU cluster. The bottleneck is the computation of many arbitrary three-dimensional projections. The communication overhead in

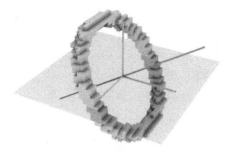

Figure 6.1: A group g of voxels with same rounded distance r from the axis of symmetry (red) and rounded position d along the axis of symmetry. Both r and d are rounded to multiples of 3, so the ring has a width of about 3 voxels in both dimensions. Here, the axis of symmetry is inclined about $57°$ with respect to the image plane (pale blue).

the cluster as well as the limited GPU memory prevent scaling to resolutions much beyond 512^3 voxels. In contrast, the method presented here computes only a single, axis-aligned projection, greatly reducing the required amount of memory and computation time. Since this obviates the need for a distributed implementation, it does not incur the associated communication overhead and scales well with increasing resolution. The axis-aligned projection leads to a more favorable memory access pattern, especially in a parallelized implementation. As a result, the proposed method works efficiently on a single commodity PC.

In addition, the method presented in Chapter 4 effectively penalizes the deviation of a voxel from symmetry with the ℓ_2-norm of the deviation. This favors solutions where many voxels deviate from symmetry by a small amount, leading to streaking artifacts as well as rather flat intensity distributions that convey only a limited impression of depth. In the method presented here, in contrast, the penalization effect is that of an ℓ_1-norm, producing more localized and pronounced asymmetric features and a more intense impression of depth.

6.3 Algorithm

The optimization algorithm presented in this chapter finds a *maximally symmetric* volume $\mathbf{x}$ subject to a given image $\mathbf{y}$ by solving a group sparsity problem of the form

$$\arg\min_{\mathbf{x}} \frac{1}{2} \left\| \frac{1}{\sqrt{n_z}} \mathbf{P}\mathbf{x} - \mathbf{y} \right\|_2^2 + \lambda \sum_{g \in G} |g| \max \mathbf{x}_{[g]} \quad \text{s.t.} \quad \mathbf{x} \geq 0 . \quad (6.1)$$

The normalization factor $\frac{1}{\sqrt{n_z}}$, where n_z is the number of voxels along the z axis, is chosen such that $(\frac{1}{\sqrt{n_z}}\mathbf{P})(\frac{1}{\sqrt{n_z}}\mathbf{P})^{\mathsf{T}} = \mathbb{I}$. This normalization improves the convergence of the optimization algorithm but bears no physical significance.

As in Chapter 4, the data term, $\frac{1}{2} \left\| \frac{1}{\sqrt{n_z}}\mathbf{P}\mathbf{x} - \mathbf{y} \right\|_2^2$, enforces compatibility of the volume with the observed image. In particular, it fixes the integral over $\mathbf{x}$ along each viewing ray. The regularizer

$\lambda \sum_{g \in G} |g| \max \mathbf{x}_{[g]}$, a weighted $\ell_{1,\infty}$-norm, penalizes the largest intensity value in each group. This means that intensity becomes concentrated on as few groups as possible while satisfying the data term constraints, and voxels within the same group tend to have similar intensities. Scaling by $|g|$, the number of elements in the group, is necessary to avoid biasing the solution towards larger groups, where otherwise more intensity could be deposited with only one voxel penalized. The regularization factor λ gives control over the allowed deviation from the observational data in exchange for a more symmetric result. Finally, the constraint $\mathbf{x} \geq 0$ enforces the result to be physically plausible in the sense that no negative emission can occur. The resulting volume $\mathbf{x}$ is, in a certain sense, *as symmetric as possible* while being compatible with the data.

As in Chapter 5, the FISTA algorithm is used to solve the optimization problem (6.1). However, the proximal mapping of the ℓ_∞-norm for $\mathbf{x} \geq 0$ can be computed more efficiently by adapting an $\mathcal{O}(n)$ algorithm for projections onto the ℓ_1-ball [DSSSC08] (cf. Section 2.3.3). Complete pseudocode for the proximal mapping is found in Algorithm 3. Since the projections are independent for each group, they are performed in parallel for maximum performance. The weighting with the respective cardinality of the group is achieved by setting $\beta = \lambda |g|$.

Due to the short computation time of the proposed method, intermediate results can constantly be monitored by the user in an interactive volume renderer, and the computation can be stopped as

---

Algorithm 3 Computation of $p^+_{\beta\|\cdot\|_\infty}(\mathbf{x}_{[g]})$ in $\mathcal{O}(n)$ expected time.

$\bar{\mathbf{x}}_{[g]} \leftarrow \max(\bar{\mathbf{x}}_{[g]}, 0)$
if $\sum \bar{\mathbf{x}}_{[g]} \leq \beta$ **then**
    return 0
end if
$u \leftarrow \{u_j \in \bar{\mathbf{x}}_{[g]}\}$
$n \leftarrow 0$
while u is not empty **do**
    choose a random element u_l from u
    $u_< \leftarrow \{u_j \in u : u_j < u_l\}$
    $u_\geq \leftarrow \{u_j \in u : u_j \geq u_l\}$
    if $\sum u_\geq - (n + |u_\geq|)u_l < \beta$ **then**
        $\beta \leftarrow \beta - \sum u_\geq$
        $n \leftarrow n + |u_\geq|$
        $u \leftarrow u_<$
    else
        $u \leftarrow u_\geq \setminus \{u_l\}$
    end if
end while
return $\min(\bar{\mathbf{x}}_{[g]}, -\beta/n)$

---

soon as satisfactory quality is reached, which is often after as few as 20 iterations. In an automated pipeline, the algorithm can be set to stop after a fixed number of iterations, or when the relative difference $\left\|\mathbf{x}^{(k)} - \mathbf{x}^{(k-1)}\right\|_2 / \left\|\mathbf{x}^{(k)}\right\|_2$ between the results of subsequent iterations falls below a specified threshold (cf. Figure 6.3).

6.4 Results

The method is evaluated on several planetary nebulae with approximate axial symmetry. False-color images of the nebulae were downloaded from several internet resources (e.g., http://hubblesite.org). The images were rotated to align the symmetry axis with an image axis (dashed red lines, Figures 6.2 and 6.4 to 6.11) to create an optimal memory access pattern during reconstruction. Where necessary, stars were removed manually; this is indicated in the respective figures. To assign voxels to groups, the positions of their centers were transformed into cylindrical coordinates aligned with the axis of symmetry. The radial and axial coordinates were then divided by the radial and axial bin width, respectively, and rounded to the nearest integer. The tuple of rounded radial and axial coordinates uniquely determines the group for each voxel. In the experiments, both bin widths were set to the size of one voxel. As in Chapter 4, the three color channels were reconstructed independently. To make the results comparable, the algorithm was run for 100 iterations with $\lambda = 0.1$ in all cases. All experiments were performed on a 4-core Intel® Core™ i7-960 CPU.

Figure 6.2(a) shows the "Butterfly Nebula" M2–9, a typical bipolar nebula. The axis of symmetry was assumed to lie horizontally within the image plane, and an automatic reconstruction was performed. The resulting model, Figure 6.2(b), almost exactly reproduces the original

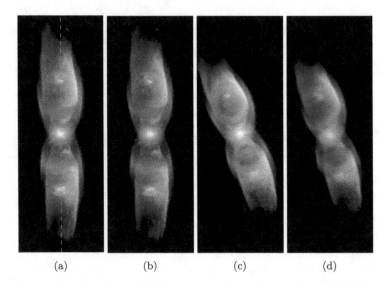

(a)　　　　(b)　　　　(c)　　　　(d)

Figure 6.2: The Butterfly Nebula M2–9, located more than 2 000 light-years from Earth, is a typical bipolar planetary nebula, shaped by two polar jets originating from the central binary star. From a single input image (a), the proposed algorithm produces a volumetric model based on symmetry assumptions without any further user interaction. The model faithfully reproduces the input image when rendered from the original viewpoint (b). Novel views (c) preserve more detail than those created in Chapter 4 (d), and exhibit greater temporal consistency when animated.

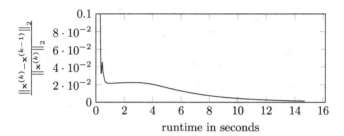

Figure 6.3: Convergence behavior for the reconstruction of M2–9 (Figure 6.2). The relative distance between subsequent iterates is plotted against the accumulated runtime.

image when rendered from the original viewpoint. Renderings from novel views, Figure 6.2(c), appear smooth and plausible.

Figure 6.3 shows the relative difference between subsequent iterates plotted over the accumulated runtime. After 100 iterations (about 14.7 s), it has dropped to a small fraction of its initial value, and no further change is visible in the reconstructed volume. For comparison, in Chapter 4, the reconstruction of M2–9 required two to eight hours (for 128 to 512 virtual projections, respectively) on a 64 GPU compute cluster at the same resolution.

For the "Ant Nebula" Mz 3, Figure 6.4(a), the inclinations of its several main axes with respect to the sky plane have been estimated at a range of 10° to 30° [MW85]. Assuming an inclination of 30°, the algorithm produces a faithful model, Figure 6.4(c), in a little more than two minutes from an image with manually removed stars,

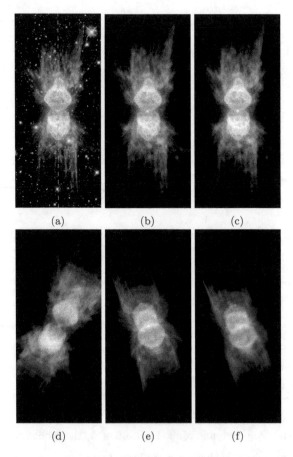

(a)   (b)   (c)

(d)   (e)   (f)

Figure 6.4: Mz 3, the so-called "Ant Nebula" (a), is a planetary nebula
with a complex composite morphology. After removing
the surrounding stars by manual editing (b), the proposed
algorithm reconstructed the $235 \times 561 \times 460$ voxel model
(c) in about 130 s. (d) and (e) show a view orthogonal to
the symmetry axis and a random novel view, respectively,
while (f) shows the novel view for the model reconstructed
in Chapter 4 for comparison.

Figure 6.4(b). The relatively long runtime is due in part to the less fortunate memory access pattern for inclined rings (for comparison, the runtime without inclination is about 51 s). Novel views of the model, Figures 6.4(d) and 6.4(e), show that in this case, the inclined projection contained enough information for a plausible reconstruction. However, for nebulae with larger inclination, the emission from different groups soon becomes too intermingled for a reconstruction from symmetry assumptions alone (cf. Figure 6.11).

Additional reconstruction results are shown for the Red Rectangle Nebula (HD 44179, Figure 6.5), a protoplanetary nebula; the Spirograph Nebula (IC 418, Figure 6.6), a planetary nebula; NGC 6826 (Figure 6.7), a planetary nebula with a bright central star and two supersonic jets; the Saturn Nebula (NGC 7009, Figure 6.8), a popular, complex-shaped planetary nebula; and the Calabash Nebula (Figure 6.9), a protoplanetary nebula with curiously dissimilar lobes. Table 6.1 gives an overview of the sizes of all reconstructed volumes and the respective runtimes. The angle shown in the second column represents the supposed inclination of the symmetry axis with respect to the image plane. To investigate the behavior of the algorithm for very large input images, the Butterfly Nebula M2–9 was again reconstructed at the largest resolution available on http://hubblesite.org (664 × 2824 pixels after rotation and cropping). However, the 3.5 GB volume could not be rendered using a GPU raycaster due to limited memory.

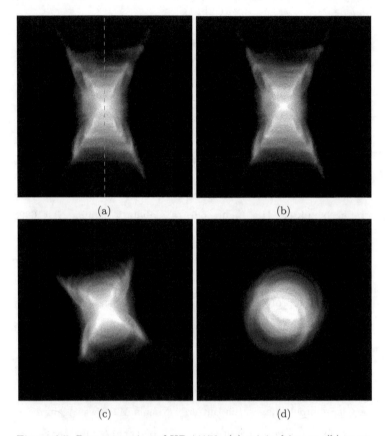

(a) (b)

(c) (d)

Figure 6.5: Reconstruction of HD 44179: (a) original image, (b) reconstruction rendered from original viewpoint, (c)–(d) novel views.

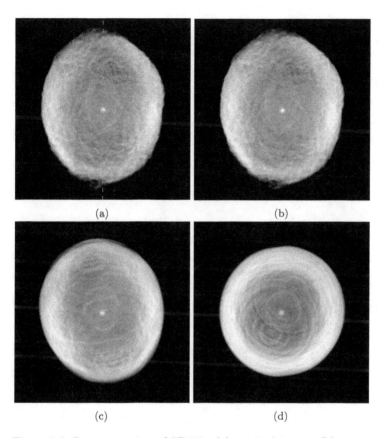

(a)   (b)

(c)   (d)

Figure 6.6: Reconstruction of IC 418: (a) original image, (b) reconstruction rendered from original viewpoint, (c)–(d) novel views.

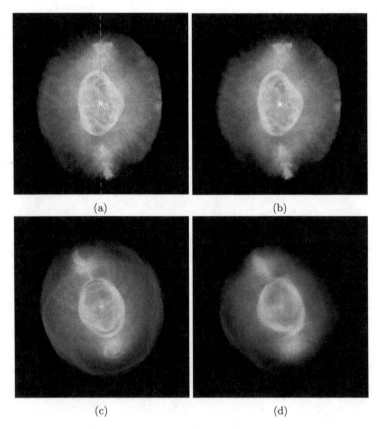

(a) (b)

(c) (d)

Figure 6.7: Reconstruction of NGC 6826: (a) original image, (b) reconstruction rendered from original viewpoint, (c) novel view and (d) comparison to Chapter 4.

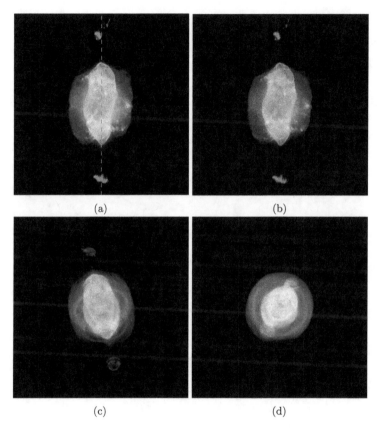

(a)   (b)

(c)   (d)

Figure 6.8: Reconstruction of NGC 7009: (a) original image, (b) reconstruction rendered from original viewpoint, (c)–(d) novel views.

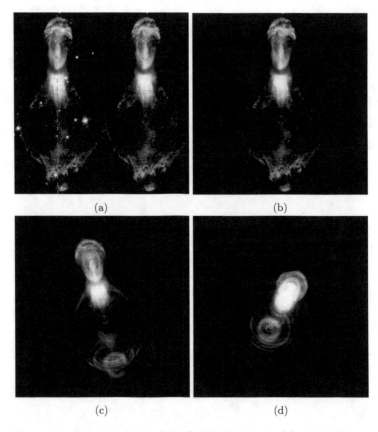

(a)   (b)

(c)   (d)

Figure 6.9: Reconstruction of the Calabash Nebula: (a) original image and edited version with stars removed, (b) reconstruction rendered from original viewpoint, (c)–(d) novel views.

Table 6.1: Reconstruction times for different data sets.

object	angle	volume size	runtime
Calabash	0°	240 × 440 × 240	42 s
HD 44179	0°	340 × 512 × 340	118 s
IC 418	0°	350 × 460 × 350	111 s
M2–9	0°	122 × 512 × 122	15 s
M2–9	0°	664 × 2824 × 664	3080 s
M 57	90°	356 × 356 × 512	245 s
Mz 3	30°	235 × 512 × 460	130 s
NGC 6302	0°	277 × 405 × 277	53 s
NGC 6826	0°	411 × 512 × 411	176 s
NGC 7009	0°	230 × 512 × 230	45 s

When the results are animated, it becomes apparent that in Chapter 4, rotations around the axis of symmetry often produced visible discontinuities, while the results of the proposed method typically show a much smoother transition.

6.5 Limitations

The algorithm attains its limits wherever any of its assumptions are violated. For example, the planetary nebula NGC 6302, Figure 6.10, contains unusual amounts of dust as well as many asymmetric finger-like structures in the outer lobes. The original projection, Figure 6.10(b), faithfully reproduces the observed image; however, novel views, Figures 6.10(c) and 6.10(d), do not contain the structures one would have expected by looking at the image.

The symmetry axis of the Ring Nebula M 57, Figure 6.11(a), almost exactly faces Earth. This makes it impossible to recover its

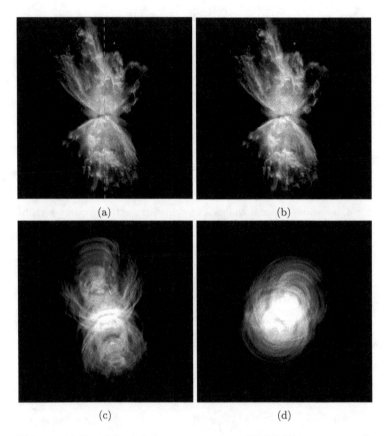

Figure 6.10: Partially failed reconstruction of NGC 6302, an unusually complex and dust-rich planetary nebula: (a) original image, (b) reconstruction rendered from original viewpoint, (c)–(d) novel views.

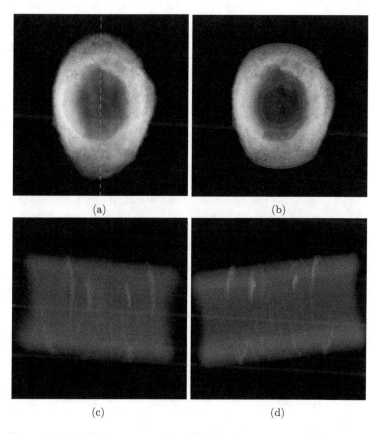

Figure 6.11: Failed reconstruction of M 57, whose axis points almost directly towards Earth, making symmetry-based reconstruction impossible: (a) original image, (b) reconstruction rendered from original viewpoint, (c)–(d) novel views.

three-dimensional structure from a single image using only symmetry assumptions. Consequently, the reconstructed volume is practically unusable, Figures 6.11(c) and 6.11(d). In addition, the regularizing term attenuates the outer regions of the nebula, Figure 6.11(b). The stair-step artifacts are due to intensity discretization in the renderer.

For all axisymmetric reconstructions, the view along the axis of symmetry is only weakly constrained by the input image. It therefore depends mostly on the characteristics of the reconstruction algorithm and reveals typical artifacts that are not easily recognized in other projections. In the reconstruction of M2–9 using the proposed method, artifacts appear in the form of radial banding due to the discrete radial groups, Figure 6.12(a). They are somewhat more obvious when displayed with a logarithmic intensity scale, Figure 6.12(b). In Chapter 4, in contrast, artifacts are present in the form of streaks, Figure 6.12(c), which become even more obvious on a logarithmic scale, Figure 6.12(d), or when animated. These streaks are produced by the discretization of projection directions.

6.6 Conclusion

This chapter has presented a novel algorithm for the reconstruction of approximately symmetric volumetric phenomena, like many astronomical nebulae, from single images. While the approach was demonstrated on emissive phenomena, it can also be applied to absorbing objects

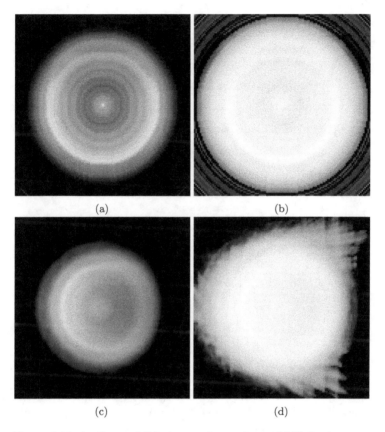

(a)   (b)

(c)   (d)

Figure 6.12: Artifacts visible in reconstructions of M2–9 when rendered from a viewpoint on the axis: proposed algorithm with (a) linear and (b) logarithmic color mapping, and the algorithm from Chapter 4 with (c) linear and (d) logarithmic color mapping. Note the radial banding in the proposed result, and the streaks in the prior work.

by transforming the problem to a negative logarithmic scale; more complex linear image formation models can be substituted as well.

The proposed method avoids typical artifacts such as streaks and unrealistic discontinuities during viewpoint changes. However, some amount of radial banding can be discerned. This could, in principle, be reduced by assigning each voxel to multiple adjacent groups with appropriate weighting factors. However, since this problem is not group separable, it requires a different and presumably more time-consuming algorithm. A possible solution would be to minimize the sum of two regularization terms

$$\arg\min_{\mathbf{x},\hat{\mathbf{x}}} \sum_{g \in G} |g| \max \mathbf{x}_{[g]} + \sum_{\hat{g} \in \hat{G}} |\hat{g}| \max \hat{\mathbf{x}}_{[\hat{g}]} \qquad (6.2)$$

subject to

$$\begin{pmatrix} \mathbf{P} \\ \mathbb{I} \end{pmatrix} \mathbf{x} + \begin{pmatrix} \mathbf{P} \\ -\mathbb{I} \end{pmatrix} \hat{\mathbf{x}} = \begin{pmatrix} 2\mathbf{y} \\ 0 \end{pmatrix} \qquad (6.3)$$

with different group assignments G and $\hat{G}$, each of which is separable. This could be achieved with an appropriate algorithm (e.g., a generalized ADMM, cf. Section 2.2.4). An overlapping group lasso algorithm [Yu13a; ZRY09] could also be used to solve the problem directly even for overlapping groups. Alternatively, by using a particle-based reconstruction approach [GKHH12], the discretization problem could possibly be circumvented completely at the expense of increased runtime.

The method presented in this chapter generates plausible models for axisymmetric objects and can in principle be extended to objects with more complicated types of symmetry by specifying a custom symmetry model. But perhaps most importantly, because only a single projection needs to be computed, the proposed approach outperforms the tomographic approach presented in Chapter 4 by several orders of magnitude in terms of computation time while requiring only a fraction of the memory. The remaining projection can be aligned with the voxel grid, making it extremely cheap to compute, obviating the need for GPU acceleration and the associated memory limitations. Because of these improvements, the proposed method for the first time allows content creators to perform automatic reconstructions in high quality without any specialized hardware, expert knowledge or modeling experience.

7 Conclusion

In my dissertation I have demonstrated through various examples that regularized optimization methods are a valuable, flexible tool with interesting applications in computer graphics, physics, and other fields. By suitable abstraction, problems that look unrelated at first— like interferometric image reconstruction and image-based volumetric modeling—can be elegantly represented within a single, consistent mathematical framework. This framework can then be used to solve all of these problems uniformly, allowing for efficient reuse not only of algorithms and workflows, but also of the associated theoretical formalisms and convergence proofs.

I have shown that through the choice of appropriate data terms and regularizers, the range of application of compressed sensing-inspired reconstruction techniques can be extended well beyond the propositions of compressed sensing theory: even when *reconstruction* is impossible from a highly incomplete set of data, it is often possible to automatically generate a *plausible model* using the very same class of algorithms otherwise used for reconstruction. In this case, the quality of the model is particularly dependent on the regularization term, which has to capture comprehensively the a priori assumptions about the model while being efficient to compute and incoherent to the information already present in the data.

As examples of reconstruction problems, I have studied the reconstruction of radio interferometric imagery from incomplete Fourier measurements in both the static and time-dependent case. For the static case, I have shown that although compressed sensing theory only guarantees certain reconstruction properties for *random* Fourier sampling patterns, the inherently non-random sampling patterns arising from real-world interferometers are on par in terms of reconstruction quality with random patterns of similar characteristics, and are even superior to uniform random distributions.

For the time-dependent case, I have proposed an algorithm to promote spatial sparsity of the temporal variation. In contrast to previous work, it allows for the reconstruction of erratically as well as continuously varying sources. Numerical experiments show that the method outperforms prior approaches in data-starved scenarios with sparse temporal variation, and otherwise yields comparable quality.

The applicability of sparsity-inducing methods to modeling problems is illustrated by a method to create volumetric models of astronomical nebulae from single images. I have introduced an approach to promote approximate axial or spherical symmetry by means of virtual projections, thereby resolving the ambiguity of depth. In contrast to previous work, this approach allows for small deviations from perfect symmetry, so that the models exhibit a much higher degree of realism. In addition, their resolution surpasses that of prior results. Due to these features, models generated automatically by the proposed method have found their way into commercial planetarium software by different vendors. At the time of this writing, the list includes Evans & Sutherland *Digistar*™ [Dig], SCISS *Uniview*™ [Uni], and RSA Cosmos *SkyExplorer*™ [Sky]. The models are also currently being integrated in desktop and smartphone applications.

Finally, by transferring findings from the group sparsity algorithm for interferometric reconstruction, I have devised a group sparsity-based regularization method to promote arbitrary symmetries in volumetric modeling. Because this allows limiting the number of projections to just one, which can additionally be aligned with the voxel grid, the computation time is reduced by several orders of magnitude with respect to the prior method, without loss in overall model quality. Because this approach does not depend on graphics hardware with limited memory resources, it is able to produce volumetric models of unprecedented resolution.

The general flexibility of regularized optimization approaches allows for a multitude of extensions to be incorporated into the present framework. Some fit rather naturally: for example, multi-frequency, time-resolved interferometric imaging could be implemented directly in terms of the group sparsity methods presented in Chapter 5. Distributed and incremental algorithms [LWSM14] may help in handling the increasing amounts of data caused by the additional frequency dimension. Other concepts fit well into the mathematical optimization framework but require customized algorithms because the energy terms are difficult to minimize using standard methods: for example, texture optimization methods [KEBK05; KFCO+07] could be used to generate synthetic detail for nebula models, and fluid control methods [FL04; MTPS04] would allow for automated reconstruction of asymmetrical astronomical nebulae. Eventually, as the resolution of the model, number of dimensions, and complexity of the objective function increase, alternative representations and probabilistic algorithms [GKHH12] become worth considering.

The work presented in this dissertation has spawned new research in the field of interferometric reconstruction [ACTW14; Har13; PVGW12; Rau12; Sch12; SWM+14; WMA+13] as well as volumetric modeling [Ken13]. It has also inspired own work on mesh animation [NVW+13] and novel optimization algorithms [LSW14; LWSM14]. Due to the universality of the regularized optimization approach and the ubiquity of reconstruction problems, there is hardly an end in sight to further work in this area. But while the research community for reconstruction problems is well established, the use of such methods for automatic, data-based modeling is only just emerging. With new methods for encoding our knowledge about the world in more and more elaborated regularization schemes and novel algorithms able to solve more and more complex problems, I am curious and excited to see what other problems in 3D reconstruction, scene understanding, and other, yet unforeseen areas of computer graphics will be tackled in this way in the future.

Bibliography

[ACTW14]   A. Auría, R. Carrillo, J.-P. Thiran, and Y. Wiaux.
            „Tensor optimization for optical-interferometric imag-
            ing". In: *Monthly Notices of the Royal Astronomical
            Society* 437.3 (2014), pp. 2083–2091.

[AFWMM08]   J. Aja Fernández, S. Wenger, C. Morisset, and M. Mag-
            nor. *Algebraic 3D Reconstruction of Planetary Nebulae.*
            Tech. rep. 7. Institut für Computergraphik, TU Braun-
            schweig, 2008.

[AHGS06]   S. Alexandrov, T. Hillman, T. Gutzler, and D. Samp-
            son. „Synthetic aperture Fourier holographic optical
            microscopy". In: *Physical Review Letters* 97.16 (2006),
            pp. 168102-1-4.

[AIH+08]   B. Atcheson, I. Ihrke, W. Heidrich, A. Tevs, D. Bradley,
            M. Magnor, and H.-P. Seidel. „Time-resolved 3D Cap-
            ture of Non-stationary Gas Flows". In: *ACM Trans-*

actions on Graphics (Proc. SIGGRAPH Asia) 27.5 (2008), pp. 132–1–10.

[Aip]   URL: http://aips.nrao.edu/.

[AMR+98]   J. Armstrong, D. Mozurkewich, L. Rickard, D. Hutter, J. Benson, P. Bowers, N. Elias II, C. Hummel, K. Johnston, D. Buscher, J. Clark III, L. Ha, L.-C. Ling, N. White, and R. Simon. „The Navy prototype optical interferometer". In: *The Astrophysical Journal* 496.1 (1998), pp. 550–571.

[AW87]   J. Amanatides and A. Woo. „A fast voxel traversal algorithm for ray tracing". In: *Proc. Eurographics* (1987), pp. 3–10.

[BAI+09]   K. Berger, B. Atcheson, I. Ihrke, W. Heidrich, and M. Magnor. „Tomographic 4D Reconstruction of Gas Flows in the Presence of Occluders". In: *Proc. Vision, Modeling and Visualization.* 2009, pp. 29–36.

[Bal04]   B. Balick. „NGC 6543. I. Understanding the Anatomy of the Cat's Eye". In: *The Astronomical Journal* 127.4 (2004), pp. 2262–2268.

[Bar07]   R. Baraniuk. „Compressive sensing". In: *IEEE Signal Processing Magazine* 24 (2007), pp. 118–121.

[BBL+07]   K. Bredies, T. Bonesky, D. A. Lorenz, and P. Maass. „A Generalized Conditional Gradient Method for Non-Linear Operator Equations with Sparsity Constraints". In: *Inverse Problems* 23.5 (2007), pp. 2041–2058.

[BF02]   B. Balick and A. Frank. „Shapes and shaping of planetary nebulae". In: *Annual Review of Astronomy and Astrophysics* 40.1 (2002), pp. 439–486.

[BF08]   E. van den Berg and M. Friedlander. „Probing the Pareto frontier for basis pursuit solutions". In: *SIAM Journal on Scientific Computing* 31.2 (2008), pp. 890–912.

[BKW08]   K. Bürger, J. Krüger, and R. Westermann. „Direct volume editing". In: *IEEE Transactions on Visualization and Computer Graphics* 14.6 (2008), pp. 1388–1395.

[BPC+11]   S. Boyd, N. Parikh, E. Chu, B. Peleato, and J. Eckstein. „Distributed optimization and statistical learning via the alternating direction method of multipliers". In: *Foundations and Trends in Machine Learning* 3.1 (2011), pp. 1–122.

[BRA+11]   K. Berger, K. Ruhl, M. Albers, Y. Schröder, A. Scholz, S. Guthe, and M. Magnor. „The capturing of turbulent gas flows using multiple Kinects". In: *Proc. IEEE International Conference on Computer Vision (Workshop*

on Consumer Depth Cameras for Computer Vision).
2011, pp. 1108–1113.

[BSO08]   J. Bobin, J.-L. Starck, and R. Ottensamer. „Compressed Sensing in Astronomy". In: *IEEE Journal of Selected Topics in Signal Processing* 2 (2008), pp. 718–726.

[BT09]   A. Beck and M. Teboulle. „A fast iterative shrinkage-thresholding algorithm for linear inverse problems". In: *SIAM Journal on Imaging Sciences* 2.1 (2009), pp. 183–202.

[BVN07a]   A. Bolstad, B. van Veen, and R. Nowak. „Space-time sparsity regularization for the magnetoencephalography inverse problem". In: *Proc. IEEE International Symposium on Biomedical Imaging.* 2007, pp. 984–987.

[BVN07b]   A. Bolstad, B. van Veen, and R. Nowak. „Magneto-/electroencephalography with space-time sparse priors". In: *Proc. IEEE Workshop on Statistical Signal Processing.* 2007, pp. 190–194.

[Can06]   E. Candès. „Compressive sampling". In: *Proc. International Congress of Mathematicians.* Vol. 3. 2006, pp. 1433–1452.

[Cas]   URL: http://casa.nrao.edu/.

[CBW+10] K. Choi, S. Boyd, J. Wang, L. Xing, L. Zhu, and T.-S. Suh. „Compressed sensing based cone-beam computed tomography reconstruction with a first-order method". In: *Medical Physics* 37.9 (2010), pp. 5113–5125.

[CCPW07] C. Chaux, P. Combettes, J.-C. Pesquet, and V. Wajs. „A variational formulation for frame-based inverse problems". In: *Inverse Problems* 23.4 (2007), pp. 1495–1522.

[CD09] A. Chambolle and J. Darbon. „On Total Variation Minimization and Surface Evolution Using Parametric Maximum Flows". In: *International Journal of Computer Vision* 84 (2009), pp. 288–307.

[CDF92] A. Cohen, I. Daubechies, and J. Feauveau. „Biorthogonal bases of compactly supported wavelets". In: *Communications on Pure and Applied Mathematics* 45 (1992), pp. 485–560.

[CDS98] S. Chen, D. Donoho, and M. Saunders. „Atomic decomposition by basis pursuit". In: *SIAM Journal on Scientific Computing* 20.1 (1998), pp. 33–61.

[CE85] T. Cornwell and K. Evans. „A simple maximum entropy deconvolution algorithm". In: *Astronomy and Astrophysics* 143 (1985), pp. 77–83.

[Cel] URL: http://www.celestia.info/.

[CGB08]   T. Cornwell, K. Golap, and S. Bhatnagar. „The Non-coplanar Baselines Effect in Radio Interferometry: The W-Projection Algorithm". In: *IEEE Journal of Selected Topics in Signal Processing* 2 (2008), pp. 647–657.

[Cha04]   A. Chambolle. „An algorithm for total variation minimization and applications". In: *Journal of Mathematical Imaging and Vision* 20 (2004), pp. 89–97.

[Cla80]   B. Clark. „An efficient implementation of the algorithm 'CLEAN'". In: *Astronomy and Astrophysics* 89 (1980), pp. 377–378.

[Com09]   P. Combettes. „Iterative construction of the resolvent of a sum of maximal monotone operators". In: *Journal of Convex Analysis* 16.4 (2009), pp. 727–748.

[Cor08]   T. Cornwell. „Multiscale CLEAN Deconvolution of Radio Synthesis Images". In: *IEEE Journal of Selected Topics in Signal Processing* 2 (2008), pp. 793–801.

[Cor83]   T. Cornwell. „A method of stabilizing the CLEAN algorithm". In: *Astronomy and Astrophysics* 121 (1983), pp. 281–285.

[CP11]   A. Chambolle and T. Pock. „A first-order primal-dual algorithm for convex problems with applications to imaging". In: *Journal of Mathematical Imaging and Vision* 40.1 (2011), pp. 120–145.

[CRT06a]   E. Candès, J. Romberg, and T. Tao. „Robust uncertainty principles: Exact signal reconstruction from highly incomplete frequency information". In: *IEEE Transactions on Information Theory* 52 (2006), pp. 489–509.

[CRT06b]   E. Candès, J. Romberg, and T. Tao. „Stable signal recovery from incomplete and inaccurate measurements". In: *Communications on Pure and Applied Mathematics* 59 (2006), pp. 1207–1223.

[CT05]   E. Candès and T. Tao. „Decoding by linear programming". In: *IEEE Transactions on Information Theory* 51 (2005), pp. 4203–4215.

[CT06]   E. Candès and T. Tao. „Near-optimal signal recovery from random projections: universal encoding strategies?" In: *IEEE Transactions on Information Theory* 52 (2006), pp. 5406–5425.

[CT65]   J. Cooley and J. Tukey. „An algorithm for the machine calculation of complex Fourier series". In: *Mathematics of Computation* 19 (1965), pp. 297–301.

[DAB01]   S. Davis, M. Abrams, and J. Brault. *Fourier transform spectrometry*. Academic Press, 2001.

[Dau88]   I. Daubechies. „Orthonormal bases of compactly supported wavelets". In: *Communications on Pure and Applied Mathematics* 41 (1988), pp. 909–996.

[DDM04]   I. Daubechies, M. Defrise, and C. de Mol. „An iterative thresholding algorithm for linear inverse problems with a sparsity constraint". In: *Communications on pure and applied mathematics* 57.11 (2004), pp. 1413–1457.

[DFL08]   I. Daubechies, M. Fornasier, and I. Loris. „Accelerated projected gradient method for linear inverse problems with sparsity constraints". In: *Fourier Analysis and Applications* 14.5 (2008), pp. 764–792.

[Dig]   URL: http://es.com/Products/Digistar.html.

[DJL92]   R. DeVore, B. Jawerth, and B. Lucier. „Image compression through wavelet transform coding". In: *IEEE Transactions on Information Theory* 38 (1992), pp. 719–746.

[DMF12]   A. Dabbech, D. Mary, and C. Ferrari. „Astronomical image deconvolution using sparse priors: An analysis-by-synthesis approach". In: *Proc. IEEE International*

Conference on Acoustics, Speech and Signal Processing. 2012, pp. 3665–3668.

[Don06]   D. Donoho. „Compressed sensing". In: *IEEE Transactions on Information Theory* 52 (2006), pp. 1289–1306.

[DSSSC08]   J. Duchi, S. Shalev-Shwartz, Y. Singer, and T. Chandra. „Efficient projections onto the ℓ_1-ball for learning in high dimensions". In: *Proc. International Conference on Machine Learning.* 2008, pp. 272–279.

[ECC+09]   S. Ellingson, T. Clarke, A. Cohen, J. Craig, N. Kassim, Y. Pihlstrom, L. Rickard, and G. Taylor. „The Long Wavelength Array". In: *Proceedings of the IEEE* 97 (2009), pp. 1421–1430.

[Eke03]   R. Ekers. „Square Kilometre Array (SKA)". In: *Proc. IAU 8th Asian-Pacific Regional Meeting.* Vol. 289. 2003, pp. 21–28.

[FL04]   R. Fattal and D. Lischinski. „Target-driven smoke animation". In: *ACM Transactions on Graphics.* Vol. 23. 3. 2004, pp. 441–448.

[FNW07]   M. Figueiredo, R. Nowak, and S. Wright. „Gradient projection for sparse reconstruction: Application to compressed sensing and other inverse problems". In:

IEEE Journal of Selected Topics in Signal Processing 1 (2007), pp. 586–598.

[Fou11]   S. Foucart. „Hard thresholding pursuit: an algorithm for compressive sensing". In: *SIAM Journal on Numerical Analysis* 49.6 (2011), pp. 2543–2563.

[FR08]   M. Fornasier and H. Rauhut. „Recovery Algorithms for Vector-Valued Data with Joint Sparsity Constraints". In: *SIAM Journal on Numerical Analysis* 46.2 (2008), pp. 577–613.

[GBH70]   R. Gordon, R. Bender, and G. Herman. „Algebraic Reconstruction Techniques (ART) for three-dimensional electron microscopy and X-ray photography". In: *Journal of Theoretical Biology* 29.3 (1970), pp. 471–481.

[GDLS+11]   M.-T. García-Díaz, J.-A. López, W. Steffen, M. Richer, and H. Riesgo. „A Cat's Eye View of the Eskimo from Saturn". In: *Proceedings of the International Astronomical Union* 7.S283 (2011), pp. 366–367.

[GJY11]   D. Ge, X. Jiang, and Y. Ye. „A note on the complexity of ℓ_p minimization". In: *Mathematical programming* 129.2 (2011), pp. 285–299.

[GKHH12]   J. Gregson, M. Krimerman, M. Hullin, and W. Heidrich. „Stochastic Tomography and its Applications in 3D

Imaging of Mixing Fluids". In: *ACM Transactions on Graphics* 31.4 (2012), 52:1–52:10.

[GO09]   T. Goldstein and S. Osher. „The split Bregman method for ℓ_1-regularized problems". In: *SIAM Journal on Imaging Sciences* 2.2 (2009), pp. 323–343.

[GSH11]   M. Grasmair, O. Scherzer, and M. Haltmeier. „Necessary and sufficient conditions for linear convergence of ℓ_1-regularization". In: *Communications on Pure and Applied Mathematics* 64.2 (2011), pp. 161–182.

[Har13]   S. Hardy. „Direct deconvolution of radio synthesis images using ℓ_1 minimisation". In: *Astronomy and Astrophysics* 557 (2013), A134–1–10.

[HG09]   M. Hayes and P. Gough. „Synthetic aperture sonar: A review of current status". In: *IEEE Journal of Oceanic Engineering* 34.3 (2009), pp. 207–224.

[HRH+13]   F. Heide, M. Rouf, M. B. Hullin, B. Labitzke, W. Heidrich, and A. Kolb. „High-quality computational imaging through simple lenses". In: *ACM Transactions on Graphics (TOG)* 32.5 (2013), pp. 149–1–14.

[Hög74]   J. Högbom. „Aperture Synthesis with a Non-Regular Distribution of Interferometer Baselines". In: *Astron-*

omy and Astrophysics Supplement Series 15 (1974), pp. 417–426.

[IBA+09]   I. Ihrke, K. Berger, B. Atcheson, M. Magnor, and W. Heidrich. „Tomographic Reconstruction and Efficient Rendering of Refractive Gas Flows". In: *Notes on Numerical Fluid Mechanics and Multidisciplinary Design*. Ed. by W. Nitsche and C. Dobriloff. Vol. 106. Springer, 2009, pp. 145–154.

[IM04]   I. Ihrke and M. Magnor. „Image-Based Tomographic Reconstruction of Flames". In: *Proc. ACM SIGGRAPH*. 2004, pp. 367–375.

[JLL+10]   X. Jia, Y. Lou, R. Li, W. Song, and S. Jiang. „GPU-based fast cone beam CT reconstruction from undersampled and noisy projection data via total variation". In: *Medical Physics* 37 (2010), pp. 1757–1760.

[Kas92]   M. Kass. „Inverse problems in computer graphics". In: *Creating and animating the virtual world*. Springer, 1992, pp. 21–33.

[KEBK05]   V. Kwatra, I. Essa, A. Bobick, and N. Kwatra. „Texture optimization for example-based synthesis". In: *ACM Transactions on Graphics*. Vol. 24. 3. 2005, pp. 795–802.

[Ken13]   B. Kent. „Visualizing Astronomical Data with Blender". In: *Publications of the Astronomical Society of the Pacific* 125.928 (2013), pp. 731–748.

[KFCO+07]   J. Kopf, C.-W. Fu, D. Cohen-Or, O. Deussen, D. Lischinski, and T.-T. Wong. „Solid texture synthesis from 2D exemplars". In: *ACM Transactions on Graphics* 26.3 (2007), pp. 2–1–9.

[KISE13]   O. Klehm, I. Ihrke, H.-P. Seidel, and E. Eisemann. „Volume stylizer: tomography-based volume painting". In: *Proc. ACM SIGGRAPH Symposium on Interactive 3D Graphics and Games.* 2013, pp. 161–168.

[KKP09]   J. Keiner, S. Kunis, and D. Potts. „Using NFFT 3—a software library for various nonequispaced fast Fourier transforms". In: *ACM Transactions on Mathematical Software* 36.4 (2009), pp. 19–41.

[KKS11]   N. Koning, S. Kwok, and W. Steffen. „Morphology of the Red Rectangle proto-planetary nebula". In: *The Astrophysical Journal* 740.27 (2011), pp. 1–9.

[KS05]   S. Kwok and K. Su. „Discovery of multiple coaxial rings in the quadrupolar planetary nebula NGC 6881". In: *The Astrophysical Journal Letters* 635.1 (2005), pp. L49–L52.

[KS13]   N. K. Kalantari and P. Sen. „Removing the noise in Monte Carlo rendering with general image denoising algorithms". In: *Computer Graphics Forum*. Vol. 32. 2. 2013, pp. 93–102.

[KW03]   J. Krüger and R. Westermann. „Acceleration techniques for GPU-based volume rendering". In: *Proc. IEEE Visualization*. 2003, pp. 38–43.

[Kwo07]   S. Kwok. *The origin and evolution of planetary nebulae*. Vol. 33. Cambridge University Press, 2007.

[LAM97]   A. Lannes, E. Anterrieu, and P. Maréchal. „CLEAN and WIPE". In: *A&AS* 123.1 (1997), pp. 183–198.

[LDP07]   M. Lustig, D. Donoho, and J. Pauly. „Sparse MRI: The Application of Compressed Sensing for Rapid MR Imaging". In: *Magnetic Resonance in Medicine* 58 (2007), pp. 1182–1195.

[LDSP08]   M. Lustig, D. Donoho, J. Santos, and J. Pauly. „Compressed Sensing MRI". In: *IEEE Signal Processing Magazine* 25.2 (2008), pp. 72–82.

[Lea91]   D. Leahy. „Deprojection of emission in axially symmetric transparent systems". In: *Astronomy and Astrophysics* 247 (1991), pp. 584–589.

[LHM+07]   A. Lintu, L. Hoffman, M. Magnor, H. Lensch, and H.-P. Seidel. „3D Reconstruction of Reflection Nebulae from a Single Image." In: *Proc. Vision, Modeling and Visualization*. 2007, pp. 109–116.

[LSW14]   D. Lorenz, F. Schöpfer, and S. Wenger. „The Linearized Bregman Method via Split Feasibility Problems: Analysis and Generalizations". In: *SIAM Journal on Imaging Sciences* (2014). To appear.

[LWM11]   L. Lindemann, S. Wenger, and M. Magnor. „Evaluation of Video Artifact Perception Using Event-Related Potentials". In: *Proc. ACM Applied Perception in Computer Graphics and Visualization*. 2011, pp. 1–5.

[LWSM14]   D. Lorenz, S. Wenger, F. Schöpfer, and M. Magnor. „A sparse Kaczmarz solver and a linearized Bregman method for online compressed sensing". In: *Proc. IEEE International Conference on Image Processing*. To appear. 2014.

[Max95]   N. Max. „Optical models for direct volume rendering". In: *IEEE Transactions on Visualization and Computer Graphics* 1.2 (1995), pp. 99–108.

[MFG11]   H. Monteiro and D. Falceta-Gonçalves. „Three-dimensional Photoionization Structure and Distances of Planetary Nebulae. IV. NGC 40". In: *The Astrophysical Journal* 738 (2011), pp. 174–183.

[MFPL04]   D. Mékarnia, J. de Freitas Pacheco, and E. Lagadec. „3D Structure of the Planetary Nebula NGC 7027". In: *Asymmetrical Planetary Nebulae III: Winds, Structure and the Thunderbird*. Ed. by M. Meixner, J. Kastner, B. Balick, and N. Soker. Vol. 313. Astronomical Society of the Pacific Conference Series. 2004, pp. 119–122.

[MHLH05]   M. Magnor, K. Hildebrand, A. Lintu, and A. Hanson. „Reflection Nebula Visualization". In: *Proc. IEEE Visualization*. 2005, pp. 255–262.

[MKHD04]   M. Magnor, G. Kindlmann, C. Hansen, and N. Duric. „Constrained Inverse Volume Rendering for Planetary Nebulae". In: *Proc. IEEE Visualization*. 2004, pp. 83–90.

[MKHD05]   M. Magnor, G. Kindlmann, C. Hansen, and N. Duric. „Reconstruction and visualization of planetary nebulae". In: *IEEE Transactions on Visualization and Computer Graphics* 11.5 (2005), pp. 485–496.

[ML94]   S. Marschner and R. Lobb. „An evaluation of reconstruction filters for volume rendering". In: *Proc. IEEE Visualization*. 1994, pp. 100–107.

[MS08]   J. McEwen and A. Scaife. „Simulating full-sky inter-
             ferometric observations". In: *Monthly Notices of the
             Royal Astronomical Society* 389 (2008), pp. 1163–1178.

[MSGH04]   H. Monteiro, H. Schwarz, R. Gruenwald, and S. Heath-
             cote. „Three-dimensional photoionization structure and
             distances of planetary nebulae. I. NGC 6369". In: *The
             Astrophysical Journal* 609 (2004), pp. 194–202.

[MSK+10]   M. Magnor, P. Sen, J. Kniss, E. Angel, and S. Wenger.
             „Progress in Rendering and Modeling for Digital Plan-
             etariums". In: *Proc. Eurographics Area Papers*. 2010,
             pp. 1–8.

[MTPS04]   A. McNamara, A. Treuille, Z. Popović, and J. Stam.
             „Fluid control using the adjoint method". In: *ACM
             Transactions On Graphics*. Vol. 23. 3. 2004, pp. 449–
             456.

[MW85]   J. Meaburn and J. Walsh. „Echelle observations of
             high-velocity lobes projecting from the core of the
             bipolar nebula Mz 3". In: *Monthly Notices of the Royal
             Astronomical Society* 215 (1985), pp. 761–771.

[MZ93]   S. Mallat and Z. Zhang. „Matching pursuits with time-
             frequency dictionaries". In: *IEEE Transactions on Sig-
             nal Processing* 41 (1993), pp. 3397–3415.

[MÇW05]   D. Malioutov, M. Çetin, and A. Willsky. „A sparse signal reconstruction perspective for source localization with sensor arrays". In: *IEEE Transactions on Signal Processing* 53.8 (2005), pp. 3010–3022.

[NGN+01]   D. Nadeau, J. Genetti, S. Napear, B. Pailthorpe, C. Emmart, E. Wesselak, and D. Davidson. „Visualizing stars and emission nebulas". In: *Computer Graphics Forum* 20.1 (2001), pp. 27–33.

[NV09]   D. Needell and R. Vershynin. „Uniform Uncertainty Principle and Signal Recovery via Regularized Orthogonal Matching Pursuit". In: *Foundations of Computational Mathematics* 9 (2009), pp. 317–334.

[NVW+13]   T. Neumann, K. Varanasi, S. Wenger, M. Wacker, M. Magnor, and C. Theobalt. „Sparse Localized Deformation Components". In: *ACM Transactions on Graphics (Proc. SIGGRAPH Asia)* 32.6 (2013), pp. 179–1–10.

[NW01]   F. Natterer and F. Wübbeling. „The attenuated ray transform". In: *Mathematical methods in image reconstruction*. Society for Industrial Mathematics, 2001. Chap. 2.4.1.

[PB13]   N. Parikh and S. Boyd. „Proximal Algorithms". In: *Foundations and Trends in Optimization* 1.3 (2013), pp. 123–231.

[PSB89]   R. Perley, F. Schwab, and A. Bridle, eds. *Synthesis Imaging in Radio Astronomy*. Vol. 6. Conference Series. Astronomical Society of the Pacific, 1989.

[PVGW12]   G. Puy, P. Vandergheynst, R. Gribonval, and Y. Wiaux. „Universal and efficient compressed sensing by spread spectrum and application to realistic Fourier imaging techniques". In: *EURASIP Journal on Advances in Signal Processing* 2012.1 (2012), pp. 1–13.

[Rau12]   U. Rau. „Radio interferometric imaging of spatial structure that varies with time and frequency". In: *Image Reconstruction from Incomplete Data VII*. Vol. 8500. Proc. SPIE Optical Engineering + Applications. 2012, 85000N–1–2.

[RH60]   M. Ryle and A. Hewish. „The synthesis of large radio telescopes". In: *Monthly Notices of the Royal Astronomical Society* 120 (1960), pp. 220–230.

[RMMD04]   A. Reche-Martinez, I. Martin, and G. Drettakis. „Volumetric reconstruction and interactive rendering of trees from photographs". In: *ACM Transactions on Graphics*. Vol. 23. 3. 2004, pp. 720–727.

[RV46]   M. Ryle and D. Vonberg. „Solar Radiation on 175 Mc./s." In: *Nature* 158 (1946), pp. 339–340.

[RWF+13]   K. Ruhl, S. Wenger, D. Franke, J. Saretzki, and M. Magnor. „Fine-Scale Editing of Continuous Volumes using Adaptive Surfaces". In: *Proc. Vision, Modeling and Visualization.* 2013, pp. 1–2.

[SB84]   J. Skilling and R. Bryan. „Maximum entropy image reconstruction-general algorithm". In: *Monthly Notices of the Royal Astronomical Society* 211 (1984), pp. 111–124.

[Sch04]   R. Schilizzi. „The Square Kilometer Array". In: *Society of Photo-Optical Instrumentation Engineers (SPIE) Conference Series.* Vol. 5489. 2004, pp. 62–71.

[Sch12]   L. Schwardt. „Compressed sensing imaging with the KAT-7 array". In: *Proc. International Conference on Electromagnetics in Advanced Applications.* 2012, pp. 690–693.

[Sch78]   U. Schwarz. „Mathematical-statistical Description of the Iterative Beam Removing Technique (Method CLEAN)". In: *Astronomy and Astrophysics* 65 (1978), pp. 345–356.

[Sch79]   U. Schwarz. „The Method CLEAN – Use, Misuse and Variations (invited paper)". In: *Proc. IAU Colloq. 49: Image Formation from Coherence Functions in Astron-*

omy. Ed. by C. van Schooneveld. Vol. 76. Astrophysics and Space Science Library. 1979, pp. 261–275.

[Sch84] F. Schwab. „Relaxing the isoplanatism assumption in self-calibration; applications to low-frequency radio interferometry". In: *The Astronomical Journal* 89 (1984), pp. 1076–1081.

[SD04] J. Sijbers and A. den Dekker. „Maximum likelihood estimation of signal amplitude and noise variance from MR data". In: *Magnetic Resonance in Medicine* 51.3 (2004), pp. 586–594.

[SD09] P. Sen and S. Darabi. „Compressive Dual Photography". In: *Computer Graphics Forum* 28 (2009), pp. 609–618.

[SD10] P. Sen and S. Darabi. „Compressive estimation for signal integration in rendering". In: *Computer Graphics Forum*. Vol. 29. 4. 2010, pp. 1355–1363.

[SD11] P. Sen and S. Darabi. „Compressive rendering: A rendering application of compressed sensing". In: *IEEE Transactions on Visualization and Computer Graphics* 17.4 (2011), pp. 487–499.

[SDX11] P. Sen, S. Darabi, and L. Xiao. „Compressive rendering of multidimensional scenes". In: *Video Processing and Computational Video*. Ed. by D. Cremers, M. Magnor, M. Oswald, and L. Zelnik-Manor. Springer, 2011, pp. 152–183.

[SEW+13]   M. Stengel, M. Eisemann, S. Wenger, B. Hell, and M. Magnor. „Optimizing Apparent Display Resolution Enhancement for Arbitrary Videos". In: *IEEE Transactions on Image Processing* 22.9 (2013), pp. 3604–3613.

[SF78]   A. Segalovitz and B. Frieden. „A 'CLEAN'-type Deconvolution Algorithm". In: *Astronomy and Astrophysics* 70 (1978), pp. 335–343.

[SFM11]   I. Stewart, D. Fenech, and T. Muxlow. „A multiple-beam CLEAN for imaging intra-day variable radio sources". In: *Astronomy and Astrophysics* 535 (2011), A81–1–9.

[SJM68]   G. Swenson Jr. and N. Mathur. „The interferometer in radio astronomy". In: *Proceedings of the IEEE* 56 (1968), pp. 2114–2130.

[SKW+11]   W. Steffen, N. Koning, S. Wenger, C. Morisset, and M. Magnor. „Shape: A 3D Modeling Tool for Astrophysics". In: *IEEE Transactions on Visualization and Computer Graphics* 17.4 (2011), pp. 454–465.

[Sky]   URL: http : / / www . rsacosmos . com / en / products / software/skyexplorer-v3.html.

[SM06]   H. Schwarz and H. Monteiro. „Three-dimensional Pho-
             toionization Structure and Distances of Planetary Neb-
             ulae. III. NGC 6781". In: *The Astrophysical Journal*
             648 (2006), pp. 430–434.

[SP08]   E. Sidky and X. Pan. „Image reconstruction in circu-
             lar cone-beam computed tomography by constrained,
             total-variation minimization". In: *Physics in Medicine
             and Biology* 53 (2008), p. 4777.

[STR+06]   F. Sabbadin, M. Turatto, R. Ragazzoni, E. Cappellaro,
             and S. Benetti. „The structure of planetary nebulae:
             theory vs. practice". In: *Astronomy and Astrophysics*
             451.3 (2006), pp. 937–949.

[Suk09]   A. Suksmono. „Deconvolution of VLBI images based on
             compressive sensing". In: *Proc. International Confer-
             ence on Electrical Engineering and Informatics.* Vol. 1.
             2009, pp. 110–116.

[Sul08]   R. Sullivan. „Synthetic Aperture Radar". In: *Radar
             Handbook.* 3rd edition. McGraw–Hill, 2008. Chap. 17.

[SWM+14]   P. Sutter, B. Wandelt, J. McEwen, E. Bunn, A. Karakci,
             A. Korotkov, P. Timbie, G. Tucker, and L. Zhang.
             „Probabilistic image reconstruction for radio interfer-
             ometers". In: *Monthly Notices of the Royal Astronomi-
             cal Society* 438.1 (2014), pp. 768–778.

[TBI97]   L. Trefethen and D. Bau III. *Numerical linear algebra.* Vol. 50. SIAM, 1997.

[TG07]   J. Tropp and A. Gilbert. „Signal recovery from random measurements via orthogonal matching pursuit". In: *IEEE Transactions on Information Theory* 53 (2007), pp. 4655–4666.

[TNC09]   J. Tang, B. Nett, and G.-H. Chen. „Performance comparison between total variation (TV)-based compressed sensing and statistical iterative reconstruction algorithms". In: *Physics in Medicine and Biology* 54.19 (2009), pp. 5781–5804.

[TWM13a]   J.-P. Tauscher, S. Wenger, and M. Magnor. „Audio Resynthesis on the Dancefloor: A Music Structural Approach". In: *Proc. Vision, Modeling and Visualization.* 2013, pp. 1–8.

[TWM13b]   J.-P. Tauscher, S. Wenger, and M. Magnor. *Audio Resynthesis on the Dancefloor: A Music Structural Approach.* Tech. rep. 19. Institut für Computergraphik, TU Braunschweig, 2013.

[Uni]   URL: http://sciss.se/uniview.php.

[VGN09]   M. de Vos, A. Gunst, and R. Nijboer. „The LOFAR telescope: System Architecture and Signal Processing". In: *Proceedings of the IEEE* 97 (2009), pp. 1431–1437.

[VGS+12]   D. Vock, S. Gumhold, M. Spehr, J. Staib, P. Westfeld, and H.-G. Maas. „GPU-Based Volumetric Reconstruction and Rendering of Trees From Multiple Images". In: *The Photogrammetric Record* 27.138 (2012), pp. 175–194.

[VKWP03]   A. Vakhtin, D. Kane, W. Wood, and K. Peterson. „Common-path interferometer for frequency-domain optical coherence tomography". In: *Applied Optics* 42.34 (2003), pp. 6953–6958.

[Vog02]   C. Vogel. *Computational methods for inverse problems.* SIAM, 2002.

[WAFMM09]   S. Wenger, J. Aja Fernández, C. Morisset, and M. Magnor. „Algebraic 3D Reconstruction of Planetary Nebulae". In: *Journal of WSCG* 17.1 (2009), pp. 33–40.

[WAG+12]   S. Wenger, M. Ament, S. Guthe, D. Lorenz, A. Tillmann, D. Weiskopf, and M. Magnor. „Visualization of Astronomical Nebulae via Distributed Multi-GPU Compressed Sensing Tomography". In: *IEEE Transactions on Visualization and Computer Graphics (Proc. Visualization / InfoVis)* 18.12 (2012), pp. 2188–2197.

[WAS+12] S. Wenger, M. Ament, W. Steffen, N. Koning, D. Weiskopf, and M. Magnor. „Interactive Visualization and Simulation of Astronomical Nebulae". In: *Computing in Science & Engineering* 14.3 (2012). Editorial article., pp. 78–87.

[WDR08] C. Wapenaar, D. Draganov, and J. Robertsson. *Seismic interferometry: History and present status*. Vol. 26. Society of Exploration Geophysicists, 2008.

[WDS+10] S. Wenger, S. Darabi, P. Sen, K.-H. Glassmeier, and M. Magnor. „Compressed Sensing for Aperture Synthesis Imaging". In: *Proc. IEEE International Conference on Image Processing*. 2010, pp. 1381–1384.

[Wen09] S. Wenger. „3D Reconstruction of Planetary Nebulae using Hybrid Models". Diplomarbeit. Institut für Computergraphik, TU Braunschweig, 2009.

[Wen10] S. Wenger. „Compressed Sensing in Radio Interferometry Imaging". Diplomarbeit. Institut für Geophysik und extraterrestrische Physik, TU Braunschweig, 2010.

[WJM12] S. Wenger, S. John, and M. Magnor. *The Parabolic Multi-Mirror Camera*. Poster at CVPR Workshop for Computational Cameras and Displays. 2012.

[WJP+09]   Y. Wiaux, L. Jacques, G. Puy, A. Scaife, and P. Van-
             dergheynst. „Compressed sensing imaging techniques
             for radio interferometry". In: *Monthly Notices of the
             Royal Astronomical Society* 395 (2009), pp. 1733–1742.

[WLHR11]   G. Wetzstein, D. Lanman, W. Heidrich, and R. Raskar.
             „Layered 3D: tomographic image synthesis for attenuation-
             based light field and high dynamic range displays".
             In: *ACM Transactions on Graphics*. Vol. 30. 4. 2011,
             pp. 95–1–12.

[WLM13]   S. Wenger, D. Lorenz, and M. Magnor. „Fast Image-
             Based Modeling of Astronomical Nebulae". In: *Com-
             puter Graphics Forum (Proc. Pacific Graphics)* 32.7
             (2013).

[WM10]   S. Wenger and M. Magnor. *SparseRI: A Compressed
             Sensing Framework for Aperture Synthesis Imaging in
             Radio Astronomy*. Tech. rep. 11. Institut für Comput-
             ergraphik, TU Braunschweig, 2010.

[WM11]   S. Wenger and M. Magnor. „Constrained Example-
             Based Audio Synthesis". In: *Proc. IEEE International
             Conference on Multimedia and Expo*. 2011, pp. 1–6.

[WM12]   S. Wenger and M. Magnor. „A Genetic Algorithm for
             Audio Retargeting". In: *Proc. ACM Multimedia*. 2012,
             pp. 705–708.

[WMA+13]   L. Wolz, J. McEwen, F. Abdalla, R. Carrillo, and Y. Wiaux. „Revisiting the spread spectrum effect in radio interferometric imaging: a sparse variant of the w-projection algorithm". In: *Monthly Notices of the Royal Astronomical Society* 436.3 (2013), pp. 1993–2003.

[WMP+10]   S. Wenger, M. Magnor, Y. Pihlström, S. Bhatnagar, and U. Rau. „SparseRI: A Compressed Sensing Framework for Aperture Synthesis Imaging in Radio Astronomy". In: *Publications of the Astronomical Society of the Pacific* 122.897 (2010), pp. 1367–1374.

[WMSM09]   S. Wenger, C. Morisset, W. Steffen, and M. Magnor. *3D Reconstruction of Planetary Nebulae Using Hybrid Models*. Poster at SIGGRAPH. 2009.

[WNF09]   S. Wright, R. Nowak, and M. Figueiredo. „Sparse Reconstruction by Separable Approximation". In: *IEEE Transactions on Signal Processing* 57.7 (2009), pp. 2479–2493.

[WPV10]   Y. Wiaux, G. Puy, and P. Vandergheynst. „Compressed sensing reconstruction of a string signal from interferometric observations of the cosmic microwave background". In: *Monthly Notices of the Royal Astronomical Society* 402.4 (2010), pp. 2626–2636.

[WRM13a]   S. Wenger, U. Rau, and M. Magnor. „A Group Sparsity Imaging Algorithm for Transient Radio Sources". In: *Proc. 2nd International Workshop on Compressed Sensing applied to Radar.* 2013, pp. 1–4.

[WRM13b]   S. Wenger, U. Rau, and M. Magnor. „A Group Sparsity Imaging Algorithm for Transient Radio Sources". In: *Astronomy and Computing* 1 (2013), pp. 40–45.

[WSK+10]   S. Wenger, W. Steffen, N. Koning, C. Morisset, and M. Magnor. *Automated Astrophysical Modeling with Shape.* Poster at Eurographics. 2010.

[WSSM09]   S. Wenger, A. Sellent, O. Schütt, and M. Magnor. „Image-based Lunar Surface Reconstruction". In: *Proc. DAGM.* Vol. 5748. Springer Lecture Notes on Computer Science. 2009, pp. 382–391.

[WWM11]   P. Wiemann, S. Wenger, and M. Magnor. „CUDA Expression Templates". In: *WSCG Communication Papers.* 2011, pp. 185–192.

[XBMJ03]   S. Xiao, Y. Bresler, and D. Munson Jr. „Fast Feldkamp algorithm for cone-beam computer tomography". In: *Proc. International Conference on Image Processing.* Vol. 2. 2003, pp. II–819–822.

[Yu13a]   Y.-L. Yu. „Better approximation and faster algorithm using the proximal average". In: *Advances in Neural Information Processing Systems*. 2013, pp. 458–466.

[Yu13b]   Y.-L. Yu. „On Decomposing the Proximal Map". In: *Advances in Neural Information Processing Systems*. 2013, pp. 91–99.

[YW09]   H. Yu and G. Wang. „Compressed sensing based interior tomography". In: *Physics in Medicine and Biology* 54.9 (2009), p. 2791.

[Zhu08]   C. Zhu. „Stable Recovery of Sparse Signals Via Regularized Minimization". In: *IEEE Transactions on Information Theory* 54.7 (2008), pp. 3364–3367.

[ZO95]   W. Zheng and C. O'Dell. „A three-dimensional model of the Orion nebula". In: *Astrophysical Journal* 438.2 (1995), pp. 784–793.

[ZRY09]   P. Zhao, G. Rocha, and B. Yu. „The composite absolute penalties family for grouped and hierarchical variable selection". In: *The Annals of Statistics* (2009), pp. 3468–3497.

Glossary

A	amplitude (radio interferometry).
$\mathbf{B}$	constraint matrix.
β	step size in proximal mapping.
$\mathbf{c}$	constraint vector.
c_0	speed of light in vacuum, $c = 299\,792\,458\,\mathrm{m\,s^{-1}}$.
d	data term.
δ	first restricted isometry constant.
∂	subgradient operator, e.g., $\partial f(\mathbf{x})$.
E	electric field strength (radio interferometry).
f	regularizer.
g	index set, used to denote a subvector $\mathbf{x}_{[g]}$.
G	set of disjoint index sets g.
I	image.
$\mathbf{k}$	wave vector (radio interferometry).
L	Lipschitz constant of ∇d.
λ	regularization parameter.
$\mathbf{M}$	measurement matrix.

n_{inner}	number of inner iterations in constrained FISTA.
n_{outer}	number of outer iterations in constrained FISTA.
p	proximal mapping: $p_f(x, \beta) = \arg\min_{\mathbf{w}} \frac{1}{2} \|\mathbf{w} - \mathbf{x}\|_2^2 + \beta f(\mathbf{w})$.
$\mathbf{P}$	projection matrix: $(P\mathbf{x})_{i,j} = \sum_k x_{i,j,k}$.
$\mathcal{P}$	probability.
$\mathbf{r}$	position vector (radio interferometry).
$\mathbf{s}$	sparse representation of signal vector.
$\mathbf{S}$	sparsity basis.
σ	noise vector.
θ	second restricted isometry constant.
V	visibility (radio interferometry).
$\mathbf{x}$	signal vector.
$\mathbf{y}$	measurement vector.

Image Credits

Figure 3.1(a) http://commons.wikimedia.org/wiki/User:Hajor.

Figure 3.1(b) NASA & ESA.

Figures 4.5(a) and 4.5(c) Model courtesy of Nico Koning.

Figures 4.1(a) and 4.6(a) WIYN/NOAO/NSF.

Figure 4.7(a) NASA, ESA, CXC, SAO, the Hubble Heritage Team (STScI/AURA), and J. Hughes (Rutgers University).

Figures 4.8(a) and 6.2(a) Bruce Balick (University of Washington), Vincent Icke (Leiden University, The Netherlands), Garrelt Mellema (Stockholm University), and NASA.

Figures 4.9(a) and 6.4(a) NASA, ESA, and The Hubble Heritage Team (STScI/AURA).

Figures 4.10(a) to 4.10(b) M. Magnor, G. Kindlmann, C. Hansen, and N. Duric.

Figures 4.11(a) and 4.1(d) J.P. Harrington and K.J. Borkowski (University of Maryland), and NASA.

Figures 4.12(a) and 6.7(a) Bruce Balick (University of Washington), Jason Alexander (University of Washington), Arsen Hajian (U.S. Naval Observatory), Yervant Terzian (Cornell University), Mario Perinotto (University of Florence, Italy), Patrizio Patriarchi (Arcetri Observatory, Italy), and NASA.

Figures 4.13(a), 6.10(a), and 4.1(f) NASA, ESA, and the Hubble SM4 ERO Team.

Figures 4.1(b), 4.1(e), 4.1(g), and 4.1(h) NASA/ESA and Hubble Space Telescope/The Hubble Heritage Team (STScI/AURA).

Figures 6.5(a) to 6.9(a) NASA/ESA and Hubble Space Telescope/The Hubble Heritage Team (STScI/AURA).

Figures 6.11(a) and 4.1(c) The Hubble Heritage Team (AURA/STScI/NASA).

www.ingramcontent.com/pod-product-compliance
Lightning Source LLC
La Vergne TN
LVHW022343060326
832902LV00022B/4213